BLOOD, SWEAT AND TEARS

An Oral History of the American Red Cross

Michele Turk (signature)

MICHELE TURK

E STREET PRESS

Robbinsville, New Jersey

Blood, Sweat and Tears: An Oral History of the American Red Cross
©2006 by Michele Turk

Published by
E Street Press
www.estreetpress.com

Cover design: Robert Aulicino, Aulicino Design
Interior design & typesetting: Liz Tufte, Folio Bookworks

Printed in the U.S.A.

Publisher's Cataloging-in-Publication Data

Turk, Michele.

Blood, sweat and tears : an oral history of the American Red Cross / Michele Turk. -- Robbinsville, NJ : E Street Press, c2006.

p. ; cm.

ISBN-10: 0-9777192-0-0
Summary: The story of the modern-day Red Cross as told through the voices of 29 current and former Red Cross paid and volunteer staff from all part of the United States.

1. American Red Cross--History. 2. Red Cross and Red Crescent--History. I. Oral history of the American Red Cross

HV577.T87 2006
361.7634/0973--dc22   0602

To Scott Swisher, M.D.,
a fifty-year Red Cross volunteer

and

my grandfather, Michael L. Ruberton
whose generosity continues to inspire me and my family

CONTENTS

We make a living by what we make;
We make a life by what we give.
—Winston Churchill

Foreword

President Franklin D. Roosevelt

It gives me the greatest of pleasure to greet here, at the White House, this splendid American Red Cross assemblage, and to give assurance that no enterprise is nearer to my heart than the work carried on in behalf of all humanity by this superb organization.

As you know, I have had the honor of being the President of the Red Cross since 1933—but my interest in the work dates back to my active participation in the Red Cross in the trying days of the World War.

Chairman Davis has spoken of the relationship that the President of the United States bears to this organization. You may have guessed that in my relationship to a great many other organizations of the Government I am inclined to judge the efficiency of each of them by the amount of trouble that it gives to me; and, the more I hear of them and from them, the more I know that there is trouble. So, for the last six years I can say that my absence from the Red Cross meetings, my seeming inattention to Red Cross affairs, proves beyond doubt the constant efficiency of the Red Cross.

Although ours is a semi-governmental agency, it does draw support from the people as a whole. Designated by Congress as the official, volunteer humanitarian organization of the nation, with specific powers and responsibilities, the Red Cross operates with independence and impartiality. It is universal in its appeal to our citizens, because everyone is welcome in its membership; and it is impartial in conferring its benefits.

When there is disaster, every agency of the United States Government is directed to cooperate with the Red Cross. Government resources and man power play an important part in aiding and restoring physical damage in communities struck by calamities. But they can never replace the humanitarian handling of the problems of the individual which is the work of the Red Cross itself.

I am especially proud of the improvement that has come during the past few years under our late Chairman Admiral Grayson and our new Chairman, my old friend, Mr. Norman Davis. I refer particularly to the coordination and cooperation which has been worked out in times of disaster among the many agencies of the United States Government and the American Red Cross today.

In floods, in fires and in hurricanes, the system of pooling our resources has been brought to a very high state of efficiency.

In time of local or regional disaster, all agencies—those of the Federal Government, of State Governments and of county and municipal Governments—know exactly what to do and when to do it. They are organized for instantaneous action. And, as you know, that action proceeds smoothly and without duplication of effort under the direction of the American Red Cross itself. And I remember, when we first tried this out in the great Ohio flood, soon after I came to Washington, I took a rather keen pleasure in putting the Chief of Staff of the Army and the Chief of Operations of the Navy under the Red Cross.

Furthermore, after the emergency of human suffering is cared for, other Government agencies step in with the systems of the Red Cross to carry on the work of rehabilitation—physical work and financial aid.

I hope the people of the country realize the splendid efficiency of these joint efforts. There is no lost motion, there is no waste of emergency or relief funds—and I think that no country in all the world has reached the standards which the United States has achieved in this respect in the past few years.

The strength of our splendid organization is in its appeal to the tenderest sympathies of our people. It embraces in its membership all races and creeds and it knows no politics. There is nothing narrow or sectional about it. All of our people find unity in one great objective, the relief of human suffering.

Happily, too, the Red Cross appeals both to the older people and to our young people. Through the Junior Red Cross, nine million boys and girls are being brought up in the tradition of service to others. The foundation being laid for these boys and girls in the Junior Red Cross, which has for its motto "I serve," may well be an important factor in the future welfare of our nation.

In its fifty-eight years of existence, the American Red Cross has also been exceptionally generous and active in extending a helping hand to our distressed neighbors. Within the past twelve months, not only have our resources of money and our resources of volunteer help been strained to the utmost in meeting disaster relief needs, such as the New England hurricane where great loss of life and property was suffered— but in generous contributions to distressed civilians in China, in Spain, in aiding the refugees in France, and in Chile where earthquakes took an appalling toll of life and left thousands of injured to be cared for.

The spirit of the Red Cross does not wane. In a world disturbed by war and fear of war, the unselfish devotion of the Red Cross to the welfare of others stands out in striking contrast to inhumane acts which have shocked our conscience in so many instances.

Yes, the task before us is enormous. Our work, by reason of its very nature, is never done. Our work never can be done while human misery exists.

That work must go bravely on. You are carrying out, and you are improving on, a great tradition.

We shall not fail because we know that all of America has been with us, is with us, and is going to be with us in the days to come.

— Speech at the Red Cross national convention in
Washington, D.C., April 15, 1939

OBTAINED COURTESY OF
JOHN WOOLLEY AND GERHARD PETERS AT
THE AMERICAN PRESIDENCY PROJECT,
UNIVERSITY OF CALIFORNIA AT SANTA BARBARA

INTRODUCTION

The Red Cross in its nature, its aims and purposes, and consequently, its methods, is unlike any other organization in the country. It is an organization of physical action, of instantaneous action, at the spur of the moment; it cannot await the ordinary deliberation of organized bodies if it would be of use to suffering humanity ... it has by its nature a field of its own.

    —Clara Barton, founder of the American Red Cross

Henri Dunant, a Swiss businessman, founded the first Red Cross society in 1863 after providing aid to soldiers wounded during a battle outside the northern Italian town of Solferino. A visionary, Dunant's dream of reducing suffering during wartime through a "spirit of brotherly love" inspired a worldwide movement. Today, there are 181 Red Cross and Red Crescent (the symbol used in Muslim countries) societies around the world, including the American Red Cross,

Clara Barton

which was founded by Clara Barton in Washington, D.C. in 1881.

THE FIRST TO THE FRONT

COURTESY OF THE AMERICAN RED CROSS

Since the society's founding, a Red Cross on a white background (the reverse of Dunant's own Swiss flag) has become a symbol of help and hope etched into the consciousness of people worldwide. In the past year alone, millions—those who received aid and those who donated time and money—witnessed what the Red Cross symbol stands for in the wake of the Asian tsunami and Hurricanes Katrina and Rita. In my first job, as a disaster specialist with the American Red Cross in Greater New York, I recall telling new

COURTESY OF THE AMERICAN RED CROSS

volunteers attending orientation sessions that the Red Cross is the second most recognized symbol in the world. "That powerful Red Cross symbol draws you in because you know someone is going to listen and someone's going to care," explains Peter Teahen, a Red Cross volunteer from Cedar Rapids, Iowa, who was among the first Red Cross staff on the scene after Hurricane Katrina in the fall of 2005. "No matter what the circumstances, it's a symbol that means there are people here who are going to help."

COURTESY OF THE AMERICAN RED CROSS

In this country the Red Cross stands alone among relief agencies as an icon of humanitarian relief, so much so that the honorary chairman of the organization is always the president of the United States. Even though it is an independent non-profit organization, the Red Cross was mandated by a congressional charter at the turn of the century to provide disaster relief and communications between soldiers and their families back home in wartime.

It wasn't until World War I broke out, however, that the Red Cross won the hearts of the American people. During the war, the number of American Red Cross members—by definition, anyone who donated one dollar to the charity—jumped from seventeen thousand to more than thirty million Americans. Among the new recruits was Ernest Hemingway, who drove an ambulance in France. Walt Disney and Ray Kroc, founder of the McDonald's chain of restaurants, both did the same, joining the Red Cross ambulance corps because they were too young to enlist.

The Red Cross permeated popular culture with poems and songs written in its honor. Even Daisy Buchanan, F. Scott Fitzgerald's most famous heroine, rolled bandages during the war in the *Great Gatsby*. But the enduring image that came to represent the organization by the time World War I ended was that of the compassionate and brave Red Cross nurse. President Warren Harding once wrote, "Perhaps of no other figure in American tradition have there been more stories written, pictures painted and songs sung than of the American Red Cross nurse. She has personified courage, sympathy and gentle strength in contrast with the brutality of war."

During the Second World War, the Red Cross became even more woven into the fabric of society. By the time the war ended, nearly every family in America had a member who had served as a Red Cross volunteer, contributed money or blood to the Red Cross, or received services from the relief organization.

While the early history of the charity is legendary, the story of the modern-day Red Cross is less well-known. In the decades after World War II, the organization earned its stripes as the country's foremost disaster relief agency, the largest civilian supplier of blood, and a leader in health and safety education.

Today the Red Cross is ubiquitous. The range of services provided by the 851 chapters runs the gamut from AIDS education to pet CPR. That's certainly the case in Connecticut, where I reside. Recently, when I hired a high school girl to baby-sit my children, she boasted that she was "Red Cross trained" in CPR, lifesaving and babysitting. My son attended Safety Town, a safety and education program for pre-kindergarten children offered by the local Red Cross chapter in Connecticut, and then chastised me when I didn't "stop, look and listen" before crossing the street. A Red Cross sign hangs on the wall of my daughter's pre-school class instructing how to perform CPR and first aid.

Nearly every day there is a Red Cross blood drive somewhere in America. And when disaster strikes, you can bet that the Red Cross will soon be on the scene. That's because the Red Cross is *always* there. In fact, one of its mottos is: *We'll be there.* "The Red Cross is like the police—you don't know it's there until you need it," says Ken Curtin, former Red Cross disaster services director in New York City, and FEMA's (Federal Emergency Management Agency) New York liaison to voluntary agencies.

My personal involvement goes back to high school, when I completed a Red Cross lifeguard training course. After college I went to work for the Red Cross as a disaster specialist at the Greater New York chapter in 1987, and after working as a journalist for several years, became a writer at national headquarters for www.disasterrelief.org, a Red Cross Web site. After 9/11, I had several conversations with the late Dr. Scott Swisher, a former member of the Board of Governors and a trusted family friend, which spawned the idea for a book about the Red Cross.

COURTESY OF THE GREENWICH CHAPTER OF THE AMERICAN RED CROSS
The Spirit of America mobile kitchen in Covington, Louisiana after Hurricane Katrina in 2005

It was a story I was particularly drawn to because it hadn't been told in my lifetime. While a pictorial history of the organization was published in 1981, the last narrative history chronicling the charity's activities dates back to the 1950s. My thoughts were echoed by former Red Cross president and CEO Marsha "Marty" Johnson Evans at the organization's 2003 national convention when she said to the assembled: "We need to tell our story." I felt as if she were speaking directly to me.

Instead of a history about the evolution of the organization from its beginning, I wanted to tell the story through the voices of the tireless volunteers and staff who make up the Red Cross. Their stories *are* the story of the Red Cross, a saga ripe with drama, glory, triumph, sadness and disappointment. So I began to interview Red Crossers—with each personal vignette more fascinating than the next, finding in their voices the dedication and spirit that is the heart and soul of the organization. The result is *Blood, Sweat and Tears.*

It is the story of the modern-day Red Cross told through the voices of twenty-nine current and former Red Cross paid and volunteer staff from all parts of the country. The stories range from that of a World War II veteran who credits Red Cross packages with keeping him alive when he was a POW in Germany to Americans who became heroes simply because they signed up for a Red Cross course and were later able to save a life to volunteers who spent an intense year in Vietnam cheering up soldiers. There is the staffer who pulled people from an automobile before the medics arrived; the mom who saved a neighbor's child when he was drowning; and the nurse who took off from her job to go half-way around the world to distribute food and supplies to the victims of the tsunami that struck the day after Christmas, 2004. Taken together, I hope these stories give readers a cohesive picture of the kinds of people who make up the organization and the range of services they provide, not only in this country but around the world.

While the people I interviewed were largely positive in their as- sessment of the organization, there are detractors. Some say the Red Cross has become too big—an unwieldy, even uncaring bureaucracy more concerned with building its coffers than rebuilding communi- ties. Disaster volunteers complain that the Red Cross doesn't provide as extensive services as they used to. Folks in the chapters complain that national headquarters has eliminated so many chapters that it has become difficult to recruit volunteers and donors. And there is con- stant tension between those who want to hold onto "Red Cross tradi- tion"—however they see it—and newcomers who want to modernize the Red Cross and shake off its stodgy image.

Stodgy or not, its long history of aid has touched the lives of millions, from disaster victims to the men and women of the armed forces, to the sick and injured who require blood to survive. I have seen firsthand how viscerally Americans respond to the Red Cross—both on the scene of Hurricane Hugo in the Caribbean, and more recently, in Louisiana after Hurricane Katrina.

All told, more than 220,000 Americans put their lives on hold to travel to the Gulf Coast in the fall of 2005 to help those affected by Hurricane Katrina, and then Rita, which slammed ashore three weeks later. In the days afterward, the Red Cross was omnipresent, as it had been during World Wars I and II. And once again, it became the organization Americans turn to whether they need help or want to help.

After an emergency, the instinct of the American public to turn to the Red Cross is incredibly strong, says Marty Evans. "People understand that through us they can be part of solving the problem," she says, "whether that is by providing financial assistance or by joining the corps of volunteers who are directly responding to the disaster." The critical services the Red Cross provided during Hurricane Katrina offered proof that 125 years after its founding, the agency remains a vital and necessary charity. "It's an amazing organization," adds Evans. "If it didn't exist I'm not sure even the most expansive minds could create it."

That doesn't mean it can't be improved—a situation that became clear after the terrorist attacks of 9/11 when the Red Cross was criticized, primarily for attempting to divert funds

COURTESY OF THE AMERICAN RED CROSS
Red Cross workers after September 11, 2001

earmarked for September 11 to pay for *future* terrorist attacks. To many people, the storied history and public image of the Red Cross seemed at odds with news reports of mismanagement. But the Red Cross has had its share of controversies throughout its history—and survived every one. September 11th is no exception.

After 9/11 the Red Cross was at a crucial juncture—its prestige, credibility and even its ability to collect blood and money were on the line. Marty Evans, who was then national executive of the Girl Scouts of the U.S.A., was tapped to be president in 2002 to help the Red Cross become more accountable and transparent to the millions who gave to it. In the course of a 29-year career in the Navy, Evans earned the rank of Rear Admiral, the second woman ever to do so.

Under Evans leadership the Red Cross struggled to regain its stature, reestablish its brand and win back the public trust. It seems well on its way to accomplishing this goal, to judge by the funds that poured in after Hurricane Katrina. Of the first $1 billion raised for victims of the hurricane, three-fourths was collected by the Red Cross, according to the *Chronicle of Philanthropy*. The organization's performance after the hurricane was criticized and its shortcomings were once again aired publicly, as is the case after many large-scale disasters. But the Red Cross has proved time again that its hallmark is resilience. As the famous N.C. Wyeth poster reads, "The Red Cross Carries On."

Through the first-person accounts in *Blood, Sweat and Tears,* one can understand why 55,000 people volunteered their time, dropping everything to travel to New York, the Pentagon and Shanksville, Pennsylvania, to help victims of the September 11 attacks. Why the organization's Liberty Fund topped $1 billion—far more than any other 9/11 charity. And why the Red Cross blood donation hotline received more than one million calls that day, dwarfing the previous one-day record of three thousand calls.

After 9/11 the country learned the true nature of New Yorkers when thousands pitched in to volunteer one way or another, de-

COURTESY OF THE AMERICAN RED CROSS
1933 N.C. Wyeth poster

fying their reputation as heartless and uncaring. Likewise, look beyond the veneer of the Red Cross and you will find—as I did—that the essence of the institution is its people. They are the reason the American Red Cross has been able to resurrect itself after every crisis.

Warren Zorek, a forty-five-year Red Cross volunteer in New York City, says that the biggest problem facing the Red Cross is that it's seen as a monolithic entity, an institution, and as such, people expect the Red Cross to be *there*, everywhere, every time. "The Red Cross has become *the Red Cross* and not its people," he explains. "The public doesn't realize that the Red Cross is mostly volunteers." Some small chapters have only three paid staff members to cover five counties—they rely on volunteers to carry out their services.

Since its founding in 1881, leaders have come and gone, the organization has been restructured repeatedly, new initiatives launched and focus groups convened to gauge the organization's priorities and relevance. But the core mission and principles of the Red Cross are steadfast. And the heart of the organization remains the unwavering devotion of loyal volunteers and staff members. Every year millions give their time and money to keep it going. Millions more donate blood in the community blood drives it sponsors everywhere. Red Cross workers show up night and day when needed at some sixty-seven thousand disasters nationwide each year, many of them house fires. What the volunteer and paid staffers do time and time again is often heroic. This book is a tribute to them at the time of the 125th anniversary and an oral history of an organization that will likely be around for another century or so.

Part I

THE RED CROSS AT WAR

Chapter 1

JOIN UP, JOIN IN:
The Red Cross in World War II

Angels of mercy, there's so much to do
The heavens are gray overhead

Angels of mercy, they're calling to you
So march with your crosses of red

March where the darkness shuts out the light
March where there is no dawn

Angels of mercy, the world's covered with night
But your mercy goes marching on
                    —Irving Berlin, Angels of Mercy, 1941

The bombing of Pearl Harbor on December 7, 1941, not only thrust the nation into war, it galvanized generations of Americans eager to serve their country. Millions of women took over defense industry jobs left vacant by men fighting the war—a job personified by "Rosie the Riveter," the fictional female factory worker. Thanks in part to Eleanor Roosevelt, a vocal proponent of women in the armed forces, tens of thousands of women joined the WACs (Women's Army Corps) and the Navy's WAVES (Women Accepted for Voluntary

Emergency Service). In addition thousands provided recreation and entertainment for the troops via the newly formed USO (United Service Organizations).

The American Red Cross enlisted its own army of volunteers to support its burgeoning wartime activities. On the home front, Gray Ladies boosted the morale of wounded soldiers sent stateside to recuperate, canteen workers fed GIs at train stations and docks, Production Corps volunteers made millions of garments, comfort kits and surgical dressings for the troops, and members of the Motor Corps—who counted Dorothy Walker Bush, President George W. Bush's grandmother, among their ranks—drove injured and sick servicemen to medical appointments.

Red Cross workers prepared more than twenty-seven million parcels filled with everything from powdered milk to cigarettes, packages that were shipped to U.S. prisoners of war (POWs) via the International Committee of the Red Cross.

The American Red Cross was not only indispensable, it was ubiquitous, with thousands more participating in Red Cross wartime programs overseas. "Everywhere I went in the European war theater—in the British Isles, in North Africa, and in Sicily—there was the Red Cross giving its services to our fighting men," wrote famed war correspondent Ernie Pyle in 1944.

As the sole agency appointed by the War Department to serve American troops overseas, the American Red Cross was the primary communication link between GIs and their families back home. All told, the Red Cross transmitted forty-two million messages between servicemen stationed in locales as far-flung as Iceland and Egypt and their families. Before America even entered the war, the Red Cross began aggressively recruiting nurses for overseas duty, mobilizing more than one hundred thousand. Once they were accepted into a branch of the armed forces, nurses became military officers with the rank of second lieutenant.

At the start of the war, the Red Cross opened several clubs in London as a respite for American troops, places where they could unwind and feel at home. By the time the war ended in 1945, there

FIGHTING MEN NEED NURSES

Sign Up at the Red Cross Recruiting Station

COURTESY OF THE AMERICAN RED CROSS

World War II poster

were Red Cross clubs in the European Theater of Operations (ETO), as well as North Africa, and the Pacific—more than eighteen hundred in total. Add to that the 150 Red Cross clubmobiles, mobile Red Cross units that reached servicemen in the field.

Seven thousand "Red Cross Girls," as they were known, were sent overseas during the war through the Club Program. Their job was to provide comfort, a sympathetic ear and, of course, donuts and coffee, to American soldiers. While the Red Cross nurse was romanticized in World War I, it was the club worker who stole the hearts of the troops in this war. "These were great young gals who had a lot of spunk and a lot of grit—we had a lot of respect for them," says James Megellas, a highly decorated paratrooper with the 82nd Airborne Division of the U.S. Army, and author of *All the Way to Berlin: A Paratrooper at War in Europe.* "They were pleasant and cheerful and they brought a touch of home just by being present."

In London Red Cross club workers survived "buzz bombs" and endured the hardships of food rations and living in blackout conditions. After the D-Day invasion, they drove clubmobiles—two-and-a-half ton GMC trucks—trailing the Allied army across Europe as they liberated France and conquered Germany. One day they would be singing and dancing in the streets with soldiers on their return from a successful mission, and the next day they might find themselves consoling GIs who lost buddies in the fighting. The dangers were immediate, from the risk of their convoy being attacked to their quarters being bombed. Some women even had to jump into trenches to escape enemy fire. Most agree that the experience was the high point in their young lives—and an adventure unlike any other they have since undergone. "It was the defining moment in all of our lives," says Eloise Riley, a clubmobile worker who was stationed in England during the height of the war.

Back home the Red Cross was also experiencing a peak. World War II heralded an era of tremendous growth for the Red Cross, whose coffers, personnel and programs swelled to unprecedented levels. The monumental war effort involved an estimated 7.5 million volunteers; the number of paid staff multiplied from 5,000 to 40,000. By 1945, thirty-six million Americans—one quarter of the country's population—had become members of the Red Cross.

The reputation of the Red Cross also soared. The organization's stature, elevated during the First World War, reached new heights. The Red Cross symbol became synonymous with patriotism and humanitarian relief here and abroad.

Famous artists like N.C. Wyeth and Norman Rockwell glorified Red Cross women on the cover of *Red Cross* magazine and on popular patriotic posters to both raise funds and recruit volunteers. Songwriter

The Greatest Mother in the World

WAR FUND 1943

Irving Berlin's *Angels of Mercy* became the official Red Cross wartime song, and Hollywood celebrities like Bob Hope and Shirley Temple made heartfelt appeals for public support.

Despite the tremendous goodwill towards the Red Cross, the organization did not escape controversy. This time the hullabaloo centered on the requirement, ordered by the secretary of war, that American troops pay for donuts and coffee at base canteens in England and elsewhere in Europe, because Allied troops paid for their food. Services in the field were still free, but some soldiers were outraged that they had to pay anything at all when they were at Red Cross clubs in the cities. The prices were well below cost—meals were about twenty cents and lodging cost fifty cents—but nonetheless, the Red Cross reputation was tarnished, and the long-held resentment of many enlisted men continues sixty years later.

Yet if there is any pattern in Red Cross history, it's resilience. The seed of its rebirth was sown during World War II itself, when the Red Cross initiated a blood program at the U.S. government's request to provide blood to injured GIs. After the war, it was converted into a civilian blood program that today supplies nearly half of the nation's blood. With its tremendous capacity for renewal, the Red Cross parlayed the wartime blood program into a vital service, helping to ensure that the organization would flourish for decades to come.

YOUR RED CROSS NEEDS YOU!

World War II posters / COURTESY OF THE AMERICAN RED CROSS

Enso Bighinatti
Washington, DC

From 1951 when he joined the Red Cross to 1975, Enso Bighinatti visited the scene of almost every major disaster in the country—including Appalachian floods, Hurricanes Agnes, Betsy, Beulah and Camille, and a Hawaiian volcano eruption and tsunami. He served as national director of disaster services from 1970 to 1975. In addition, Bighi ("Biggy"), as he was known, helped negotiate the release of more than one thousand Cuban prisoners after the thwarted Bay of Pigs invasion, and arranged for their safe transport to Miami.

From 1975 to 1981, Bighi served as undersecretary general for the International Committee of Red Cross and Red Crescent Societies in Geneva, where he directed more than 125 international disaster operations. Later in his career, Bighi served as assistant to two American Red Cross presidents, Richard Schubert and George Elsey, and he became the founder and first chairman of the National Voluntary Organizations Active in Disaster (NVOAD). But Bighi never would have begun working for the Red Cross if his plane hadn't been shot down over Italy on his thirty-eighth mission as a radio gunner in World War II.

COURTESY OF THE
AMERICAN RED CROSS

It was July 7, 1944. I was a sergeant on a B24 Liberator Bomber with the 15th Air Force in Italy. I was the radioman and gunner on a ten-man crew, and the only communication to the airfield. Our target was what we call a milk run, almost like a vacation. Bing! Bang! Boom! Drop your bombs and come back. But at the last minute they changed our target to Munich—one of the toughest and most protected targets.

We got clobbered over Munich and our plane was damaged—we were lucky not to get shot down. When you fly in formation, you have a tremendous amount of firepower. We were protecting everybody around us and they were protecting us. But once your plane is hit, you fall out of formation and you're practically a dead duck—and there's a half a dozen fighters coming at you. We were on fire after being hit, so they didn't bother with us because they figured we were going down anyway.

With all the noise and flames and gunfire—everything was happening so fast—it was like the whole world coming to an end. One or two of the engines were on fire. We were trying to make Switzerland—we were very close. We were losing altitude, the plane was out of control and the mountains were higher than we could go, so we had to bail out.

I was coming down in a parachute—I hadn't jumped before—and I was thinking back on all the training we had. I didn't think I'd ever need it, because it happens to the other guy, not you. I looked up and the parachute was way to one side in front of me and way in back of me, and I was swinging back and forth. I was going down, but it didn't feel like I was falling. I came down in a wooded mountain area. Luckily I landed in a dried out creek bed, on my rear end.

I thought the people who found us were Swiss, because they looked like mountain people, but they were German. Some German officers came over and threw us in the local jail in Mittenwald, Germany. I found out later that one crewmember did not survive.

Non-commissioned officers like me were sent to Stalag Luft IV, a prison camp near the Baltic Sea, up near the Polish border. It was a big camp, all airmen. I think they had seven or eight thousand men, maybe more. The camp got so crowded I slept on the floor of the barracks while I was there.

Most non-commissioned officers didn't have to work. The thing that drove you nuts is there is nothing to do all day and you are hungry. The bread they gave us tasted like sawdust. Broth and potatoes was the soup, maybe some onions thrown in. We got boiled potatoes in the "soup," sometimes with a little meat, and that was it—one meal a day.

What kept us going were the Red Cross parcels. The parcels had food—crackers, canned meat, powdered coffee and powdered milk, plus razor blades and cigarettes. The most important thing was the cigarettes—in those days everyone smoked. Cigarettes were the main currency in prison camp. Ten cigarettes were like ten dollars. You could buy or trade cigarettes for food with other prisoners or trade them to get a better bunk—even the guards were after them.

I think one parcel was supposed to last about one week. But we would get maybe one parcel for four people for one month, so we had to divide them four ways, depending on the supply. We'd split it up and the guy who got the shortest matchstick got the crumbs left on the table. Still, there's no question the Red Cross POW parcels saved our lives. I thank God for the Red Cross parcels. If it weren't for the parcels, we would have starved to death.

A buddy of mine, Aldo Tesconi, got shot down when he was flying on a mission with another crew. When we were flying in formation I would wave to him. I saw his plane blow up—when it exploded it almost knocked us out of formation. Any time a plane was shot down, the other crews would try to count the parachutes to see who survived. Well, we didn't see any. I thought my buddy was killed. Then I got to prison camp and the first guy I see is Tesconi. It was a miracle.

The Germans evacuated the entire camp, and we were sent on this march at the end of January 1945. We were up in the northern part of Germany. We marched across Germany in a westerly direction, away from the Russians on the offensive.

It was a grueling, killing march, just as bad as the march in the Philippines, the Bataan March. In fact, more people died on our march than during the Bataan March. When we were lucky, we'd sleep in barns or just out in the cold, and we'd huddle together to keep from freezing. It was a real cold, cold time of year, with a lot of snow. My toes were black. A lot of people couldn't walk—the guards put them in a wagon at the end of the line—sometimes we'd pull the wagon and sometimes the guards would take over a horse to pull them. A few guys lost their legs.

Tesconi and I were talking about escaping. We had been saving little crackers from the Red Cross parcels and eating the minimum, saving what we could. At one point, after we had been marching for two to three months—we started in January and it was now March—we decide to make a break for it. We had just crossed this gigantic river, the Elbe, and we were walking along this old cow path. We knew the riverbed was heavily mined and guarded. There was a slight blanket of snow and each side of the road was heavily wooded.

We had an agreement: Whoever saw the first chance, the other would follow. The path took a sharp turn to the right. We realized that the guards in front of us had their backs to us, and the guards who hadn't gone around the corner couldn't see us, so we had a little time when no one was watching. It was almost like we rehearsed it, but we didn't. We both just dove at the exact same time over the bushes headfirst and landed in the snow. The others kept walking. Tesconi and I just lay there without moving. The bushes were thick enough to protect us when the guards went by, and they didn't see us. When I look back now, we were nuts to even try it!

We were too tired to run, so we started walking. We didn't know exactly where we were except someplace in northern Germany. We decided to go in a westerly direction—because we knew we were somewhere near two main cities, Hamburg and Hanover. There's a highway between those two cities. The British had the northern part of the front, and we figured if you were commanding advancing troops, one of your targets would be to cut off that highway. So we thought it would be best to go for the highway because that's probably where we would meet the British troops.

We were keeping track of our direction by the moon and the North Star. We walked at night, in the woods, traveling on back roads, and we slept during the day. The German farmers stowed their seed potatoes in a hole in the ground under the haystacks and we used to dig them up and eat them. That's how we survived. We built fires with matches from the Red Cross parcels only at dawn when it was hazy. We lost track of time. Our walk seemed like ten years, but we were only a week to ten days in hiding.

At one point we were going through a cow path in the woods and we came upon a cabin with smoke coming out of the chimney. We knocked on the door and in our best German, we said, "Something to eat?" The man turned around and went into another room and he came back with a shotgun. We ran. He took a couple shots at us. I was hit with some buckshots. One went in my ankle and one in my elbow—they were just flesh wounds. The problem is the cuts would ulcerate—that was the worst part.

One night we came across this fairly broad stream. It was wide enough and deep enough so that we couldn't walk in it—it was too cold anyway—our feet would have frozen. It was late in the evening, so we decided to fall asleep and figure out how to get across it the next day. The next morning we could see across the stream and there was an open potato field, and way on the other side of the field was a road. We heard a rumbling noise and we could see big trucks going up the highway. Lo and behold, there were tanks and trucks and we see could the big stars—they were British trucks!

One of the tanks stopped right across from the brook. We got so excited, we jumped out of the woods and we made all sorts of noise. We must have looked like scarecrows. What clothes we had looked like rags and we weighed nothing—by then, I was down to ninety-eight pounds. The tanks pointed every gun they had at us. We said, "Don't shoot! Don't shoot!" We finally convinced them that we were POWs who had escaped. They lowered their guns and told us to go down several yards to a broken footbridge where we could get across.

And that was the beginning of our freedom. They gave us the first meal we had since we had been captured. They couldn't take us back because they were on the offensive to take Luneburg, Germany, so we had to go with their supply trucks behind the tanks to capture that city. When they took Lunenburg, they also captured an air base. A Wellington Bomber came in loaded with supplies. Tesconi and I were put on that plane to go back to England, and the next day we were told, "Your ticket back to the United States is here."

Enso Bighinatti was hospitalized in England for two weeks, where he was awarded the Purple Heart. After returning home to Connecticut, Bighi married his high school sweetheart, Mildred Genovese. After a short stint working in a brickyard, he took advantage of the GI bill and enrolled in college to get a degree in physical education so he could fulfill a lifelong dream of becoming a coach and teacher. But during his final semester at Springfield College, in Massachusetts, he was diagnosed with polio, and spent eight months in the hospital.

On a trip to Washington, D.C. the following year, Bighi and Mildred drove past American Red Cross national headquarters on Seventeenth Street. Mildred suggested that he stop in and apply for a job, since he had on numerous occasions credited the Red Cross with saving his life while he was a POW.

Several months later Bighi received a telegram from the Red Cross inviting him back to Washington. He was offered a job as an assistant field director on a military installation in Indianapolis, Indiana, but he was

COURTESY OF THE AMERICAN RED CROSS
Eastern Kansas tornadoes, 1966

soon transferred to Quantico Marine Corps Base in Virginia. His disaster services career was launched in 1952, when he became an assistant field director at national headquarters.

Bighi remained in disaster services until he retired in 1984, at the age of sixty-three, after a thirty-three year career with the organization. He continued on as a volunteer for another decade, serving on an emergency food and shelter committee made up of representatives of various non-profit groups active in disaster. "Working with the Red Cross for over forty years is the greatest thing that happened to me," recalls Bighi. "I saw all of the U.S. and most of the world, and I had the privilege of working with the most dedicated and wonderful people, both volunteers and staff."

Enso Bighinatti passed away on June 14, 2004.

Elma Ernst Fay
Westport, Connecticut

Immediately after the attack on Pearl Harbor, Elma Ernst Fay decided that she wanted to volunteer to serve her country at war. Instead, however, she left her job as a secretary at Camp Grant, a military facility in Rockford, Illinois, and reluctantly moved three hundred miles back home to Quincy, Illinois, because her only brother was being inducted into the Army, and he insisted that their mother, a widow, not be left alone.

Fay was twenty-four years old. She took a job with a local law firm, but never lost her desire to get involved in the war effort that consumed the country. Within months, Fay convinced her mother she needed to do her part, and she signed up for the American Red Cross's Club Overseas program. Although she thought about joining the WAVES or the WACS, she chose the Red Cross, in part because she was familiar with the organization. As a child she had taken lifesaving courses at the local pool, and she was a certified swimming examiner.

After training at Red Cross national headquarters in Washington, she was sent to New York in December 1942 to await orders for embarkation. The next three years would take her to England, where the Allied troops prepared for the D-Day invasion, through war-torn France, where she and the thirty-four women who reported to her, trailed closely behind General Patton's renowned Third Army into Germany, and to victory.

On December 27, 1942, from a dock in Brooklyn, I climbed aboard a British ship that looked like a ferryboat. We bunked

COURTESY OF ELMA FAY

six to a room on three-decker cots, and with all of our gear, we could hardly make it in the door. Seventeen days later we got to England.

In London, we were billeted right across from Red Cross headquarters at 20 Grosvenor Square, where the top-brass military of all countries was headquartered. The lovely park in the middle of Grosvenor Square had been taken over by Army vehicles and above it, there were two barrage balloons that looked like huge dirigibles. They were tied up all over London to deter German planes from dropping bombs.

The big bombing was over when we arrived, but we did experience an air raid a few days after we arrived. We were then staying on the sixth floor of the Park Lane Hotel in Piccadilly. I heard the siren, but my roommate didn't want to pay attention to it. When it kept going, we knew it was the real thing, so we put our raincoats over our pajamas, grabbed our handbags and went downstairs. We were scared—the bombing sounded awful. But we got in with a group of English people who said, "Oh, it's nothing at all," and they began telling us about the terrible raids the year before.

Whenever I get scared, my teeth chatter, and my teeth were chattering! The bombing went on for about an hour, and then we heard the "all clear" announced, and we were able to go back upstairs. The next morning, I was expecting to see buildings down, but nothing had been hit.

After a few weeks in London, we were assigned to a clubmobile. The clubmobile was a renovated bus, gutted out and designed with a fully equipped kitchen, with an electric donut machine, a Primus stove for heating water, counter space outfitted with two fifty-cup coffee urns and space for trays of donuts. It had a flap we could push out so the men could come up and get their donuts and coffee. In the back, we had a room with two bunk beds, paperback books and a Victrola with a loud speaker to carry the latest tunes outside while the troops were having their snack.

While we were in London, we were measured and outfitted with two uniforms—the Clubmobile uniform and a dress uniform. The Clubmobile uniform consisted of an Eisenhower jacket—the short button-down jacket, belted at the bottom, which also had epaulettes on the shoulders. We wore it over pants of the same material. The dress uniform was air force blue, and it consisted of a skirt and a fitted jacket, with epaulettes on the shoulders. We wore a cap with Red Cross buttons on the front.

The clubmobiles were named after states and cities—Baltimore, Maryland, Dallas. Ours was called Ohio. From the first day, the GIs would come into our kitchen and help us make donuts. When we pulled

COURTESY OF ELMA FAY
Serving the troops in England, 1943

up to serve the guys, a couple would always come in and take charge of serving the donuts and coffee, and we'd go outside and talk with the guys. We'd have the phonograph on all the time playing songs like *Chattanooga Choo Choo, Lily Marlene, The Last Time I Saw Paris, This is the Army, Mr. Jones* and *I Left My Heart at the Stagedoor Canteen*. Soon, somebody would start dancing.

My first assignment was in Bury Saint Edmunds, in East Anglia, a rural area northeast of London. The air corps was stationed there. One experience while I was in East Anglia sticks with me. We went to a Saturday night dance at the base, and I got paired up with a pilot named Johnny. He asked me if I would like to go up in one of the single engine open-cockpit planes. I had never been up in a plane. So he took me up on the following Tuesday, and did all kinds of flips, and it was sort of fun. But Johnny went out that Friday on a mission, and he didn't come back. And just knowing him a couple of days, and now he was dead, made me very sad.

In September 1943, I was transferred to a base in Newquay, a small town in Cornwall, in the south of England, to open a new base at the Air Transport Command. At that time, the army was just building up its forces in England and all of the men and equipment slated for the D-Day invasion stopped here for briefing. We could see the buildup, especially in Cornwall, where they brought the majority of troops. As we went down the road one day, a field would be just a field, and the next day, practically every inch of territory was taken over with troops. We also began seeing ground troops.

Once December arrived, we bought a couple of little Christmas trees. We trimmed them and kept them in the clubmobile. When we went out and served troops, we'd bring out the tree. On Christmas Eve we were with a group that had been out on maneuvers. It was getting dark, and

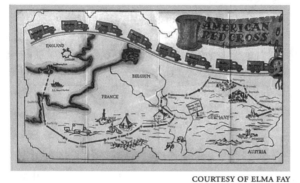

COURTESY OF ELMA FAY

The route of Clubmobile Group K

we didn't want to leave. They were so dead tired, but they looked like they needed cheering up. We asked the officers if we could stay for supper. They had a tent for their mess hall, and we took our Christmas tree in the tent and piped Christmas carols in.

Red Cross volunteers back at home had made packages—they knitted skullcaps, gloves and scarves, and they would also include candy and a little note in each package. When we got inside, we distributed these gifts to the guys and they were just so thrilled to get them. They were so happy to be with us and have a little warmth, and it just touched us so greatly—it was the most wonderful Christmas Eve I've ever spent. After about six months, we were sent up to Leicester, a city north of London, to prepare to go to the Continent. The clubmobiles were in packs of eight with two trucks with generators attached to them. I was put in charge of my group of thirty-four girls in eight clubmobiles. There was also a ninth vehicle called a cinemobile, which was a truck with a piano on board that opened up into a stage. We were all attached to the 82nd Airborne Division—their nickname was the "All American." They were top-notch, well-trained paratroopers and they had fought hard in Africa and then gone in during the invasion of Sicily.

We stayed in Leicester for three or four months and by the end of

May, we knew that the invasion was coming because there was such a big buildup, but we didn't know the date. About three days before the invasion, they closed the airfields where the men were to get on their planes that would take them to the Continent. We were on our way back to our base, and we happened to pass a field, so we stopped the clubmobile, and the fellas all rushed to the fence. They were all ready to go, with full battle gear on, helmets and guns, and blackened faces. Three nights later—the early morning of June 6th—we heard the planes roaring and we knew that the invasion had started. The next day we heard on the radio that the troops had landed, and that the men from the 505th regiment of the 82nd Airborne had jumped behind the lines of Omaha and Utah beaches in Normandy at Sainte Mère Eglise. We also heard many stories about their bravery.

We had word from London about that time to close our base at Leicester and come to the coast because every day, thousands of soldiers were being ferried across the Channel. We went down to one of the towns, where the fellas all ate a big meal before they got on their boat to go to France. We served coffee and donuts, helped dish out food on the chow line and talked to them.

We did that for about two or three weeks, until the middle of July, when we were sent back to London to await our call to go across to the Continent. That was the first time I experienced a "buzz bomb." They made me cringe, because you'd hear a buzz, and then the engine would be cut off, and the bomb came down—it would come down indiscriminately, and it was very, very scary. My teeth chattered every time the buzz bombs came—I was scared to death.

Since the buses that we had been using as clubmobiles were too big and cumbersome for driving around on the Continent, we got a clubmobile designed out of an Army GMC truck. It was really just a big kitchen, and we had no lounge in the back. But we could make coffee and donuts, and maneuvering the truck was easier than the bus. In England we had a driver, but here, we were driving the trucks ourselves, and we had to drive in blackout.

In late July we drove our new GMC truck clubmobiles down to the coast and got on the *Pearl Harbor*—to cross the Channel. We saw a calmer-looking Normandy than we had seen in the newspapers, but for miles and miles we saw debris floating in the water.

We were attached to General Patton's Third Army, the 12 Corps, when we arrived in Normandy beach in mid-August, and we stayed with 12 Corps for the rest of the war. We would make our donuts and coffee back at our base, then we would take two or three clubmobiles to one spot, so we could serve the whole group at one time.

This is the life we led for the next month or so. Below Paris, we were in Le Mans, Orléans and Sens, and we finally ended up in Nancy, in the first part of October. It was pretty fast going for the Army—General Patton had hoped to beat everyone to Berlin, so he was going like mad. But he got stopped—everybody got stopped about now—because there was a shortage of gasoline. General Eisenhower made the decision that Montgomery's troops could have it, and so that made all the Americans in France short of gasoline.

After we were in Nancy for a few weeks, we had word from General Patton asking if we would set up a clubmobile annex in town because he didn't know how long they would be there. There was another clubmobile group in Nancy at that time, and the two of us got together and set up the club, called a "donut dugout," in an abandoned theater.

Patton's niece, Jean Gordon, was in the other group and I got to know her. One night General Patton told Jean to invite another Red Cross girl for dinner and she called me. So I went over to the base and, of course, I wore my dress uniform. Patton was staying in a great big mansion and the dining room was very formal. It was an army-operated post so the GIs served dinner, which was also very formal.

That was the first time I met General Patton. He was always very smartly dressed in his military attire, and though he wasn't tall, he held himself so erectly that he was imposing. But he was very nice to us. He was soft-spoken, very gentlemanly, very polite. Because Jean and I were the only women, Patton would defer to us once in a while. There were four generals at dinner and that made me sort of shrink back—but they were nice to us also. They were having a meeting later that night, and after dinner General Patton asked, "Would you gentleman like to come to the briefing room downstairs?" Jean spoke up and asked, "Uncle George, can we come?" He said, "No, you can not." There was a general there who was originally from Quincy, Illinois, my hometown, who stayed back with us for a while, and we had a nice chat about home.

By December we got gasoline, and we began moving on. Patton was planning to go down straight through Germany, towards Bavaria, so we tagged along. At Nancy we had wonderful living arrangements, but when we got to a terrible place called Morhange, the barracks looked horrible—most of the windows were broken, and the inside was cluttered with stuff the Germans had left behind.

We got our living quarters in shape in a day and set out serving the troops nearby. Making donuts was difficult. The girls would get up at the crack of dawn, go down to the cold clubmobiles, and have donuts rolling off the machine in time for the troops' 7:00 start towards their destinations.

Christmas was coming and we were sure we were still going to be there, so everyone pitched in and we got the place all fixed up. The girls pulled out all the things they had—a pretty red scarf, a little throw rug, some pictures for the walls. One of the guys cut down a Christmas tree. We also had some decorations—we put together little garlands of colored scrap paper and we put a lot of candles around the room. Within a day, we got it to look quite cozy.

COURTESY OF ELMA FAY

Group K members Charlotte Colburn, Marianne Shellabarger and Elma Ernst, Leicester, England, 1944

We had a party and we invited the brass, and our commanding officer was quite surprised to see how we had changed the mood of the place with just a few things. The next day, two days before Christmas, *bingo*, the word came that we had to leave.

The Battle of the

Bulge had started up earlier in the month on the border between Belgium and Germany and things looked pretty bad, so Patton was called to take his troops up to Luxembourg to help. We tagged along again. Everything we had acquired—the stove, the tree, heaters and mirrors—was hanging out the back end of each clubmobile. We looked like a bunch of gypsies.

We wound up in Metz, back in France. A few days after we arrived, we were in the barracks, and all of a sudden we heard a lot of planes overhead. We rushed to the windows and saw that they were German planes, and they were bombing, and stupid us—we stayed at the windows to watch. We saw these German Stukas and they were trying to bomb an American airfield. They were practically overhead. We saw them diving up and down—it looked like a regular dogfight. They were bombing us and our ack-acks were on the ground shooting up at the planes, and I saw their planes going down in flames.

Once the Bulge was resolved, in the end of January 1945 we were on our way into Germany. The war was winding down and everything was going so fast. Often we'd go into a village that hadn't been taken yet by our troops—the German troops had fled—and the villagers would be lined up in the streets saying nasty things to us. The German people made faces and kids stuck out their tongues at us.

But you could tell the war was ending. We ran into German troops walking towards us—they were surrendering. They were surrendering in large numbers, and practically anybody could take them prisoners. We were not supposed to, but we did. They'd see our vehicles and they'd want to stop us. At that point we had acquired about five or six cars, including a command car we called Classy Lassie. It was a big, bulky sedan with a convertible top. A couple of times the Germans jumped on this vehicle and we just let them ride with us. Then we drove up to the first military installation we found, and turned them over. Some of the girls actually brought in German troops on the fenders of their cars—a couple of our girls were a little bit crazy!

We finally got to a place called Viechtach, and it was then that I had a call from headquarters telling us that the Germans had surrendered, and a truce had been signed. The Russians were in a nearby town, and there were a lot of parties—12 Corps would give a party for the Russians, the Russians would give a party for 12 Corps. We were all invited to the parties and we had a lot of fun. By the middle of June, we finally got to Regensburg, which was our last stop, and the last stop for 12 Corps, and that was the end of the tour.

I was overseas with the Red Cross for almost three years. Sixty years later, I still have fond memories. Nothing I've ever done has been as exciting, or as interesting, as those years, and no other job has given me as much freedom to make my own decisions, or as much leeway, as my Red Cross job did during the war.

Elma Ernst Fay left France with about one thousand troops and a few dozen Red Cross personnel for the voyage home. When the ship pulled into New York harbor, it was greeted by boats tooting their horns, and there were huge signs hanging on New York City buildings that read, "Welcome home Yanks" and "Thanks for a job well done." Soon after she arrived home, President Harry Truman awarded her the Army Bronze Star. After a brief stint working for the Red Cross, she began a career in fundraising and moved to New York City. She met her husband at the public relations firm where they both worked. Over the years, Fay remained in public relations, and she and her husband volunteered with many local groups, including the Red Cross Blood Bank. He passed away in 1996.

A Clubmobile Association was formed immediately after the war and Fay served as president for a few years. The group met once a year, and in 1965, they held a twentieth anniversary celebration at the Savoy in London. The association continued to have annual reunions until the early 1990s. Fay continues to attend an annual reunion of Group A, usually at Eloise Reilly's home in Westport, Connecticut, which is attended by extended families, including the children and grandchildren of clubmobilers.

Dorothy Steinbis Davis
Rockville, Maryland

When World War II broke out in 1941, the Red Cross had already begun to visit nursing schools as part of a massive effort to recruit nurses to serve in the war. When the Red Cross came to the University of Minnesota Nursing School, where Dorothy Steinbis Davis was a student, she was anxious to join. "I think I was first in line," she recalls. "Like all the other young people, I felt patriotic and wanted to help care for the thousands of wounded filling the military hospitals."

While she was still in school, Davis began teaching first-aid courses for the Red Cross and responding to disasters in Minneapolis. By the time she graduated and passed the nursing boards, she was twenty-one and old enough to volunteer for the military Nurse Corps. She signed up and as she waited, she took a job at the University of Minnesota Hospital. A few months later she was called for active duty. It was February 1944, and the Allied forces were preparing for the D-Day invasion.

Davis was assigned to the 57th Field Hospital, a mobile unit with more than two hundred staff that trailed the troops closely for eighteen months. The hospital treated the wounded at numerous battles in the European Theater of Operations (ETO), including the Battle of the Bulge. Davis, who was born and raised on a farm in South Dakota, relied on her nursing training and her hardy midwestern upbringing when times got

COURTESY OF DOROTHY DAVIS
**Lt. Dorothy Davis
wearing nurse's uniform,
Topeka, Kansas, 1944**

tough. "Most of the staff all came through the Depression, and I came from a farm area, so we were used to some pretty difficult times," she recalls.

Sixty years later, at eighty-four, Davis is still a Red Cross volunteer who has served in many leadership positions with the organization. "I believe in what the Red Cross stands for. I think the organization makes the world a better place to live, and I enjoy the work—it provides an umbrella for me to do nursing duties while volunteering," says Davis. "I just feel so fortunate to have had such incredible, interesting times with the Red Cross. It's been such a big part of my life."

The day in February 1944 when I received my army orders addressed to 2nd Lt. Dorothy E. Steinbis was one of the most exciting of my life. After attending basic training at Fort Carson, Colorado, I was sent to Winter General Hospital in Kansas City, Kansas. My assignment was head nurse of the German prisoner of war ward, which took care of prisoners brought here to work on the farms who had become ill or had been injured in farm accidents. Since my grandfather was a German immigrant, I often wondered what the prisoners must have thought of my German name—Steinbis!

In May of 1944, I received orders to join the 57th Field Hospital—the World War II version of a MASH unit. Field hospitals were the smallest of the army hospitals with about 225 personnel. The hospital was divided into a small headquarters with three medical units, or "detachments," and there were five of us in each detachment. Since we were such a small unit, we could keep up with the ever-changing battle lines. There were no helicopters to evacuate the wounded, so the closer the field hospital could be to the front lines, the more the severely wounded could be saved.

By July 1944 the 57th was fully trained and staffed, and we were excited to be going overseas. Our first assignment was Prestwick Air Field in Scotland, where we set up a holding hospital for the wounded waiting for planes to return them to a military hospital in England or the United States. Many of them had been wounded in the D-Day invasion on the 6th of June, and they were anxious and apprehensive about going home. The amputees and sight-damaged, especially, wondered how they would be received by their family and friends. We prepared them for the big trip—we changed their bandages and made sure they had their medications. Many of these men had never been on a plane before, the nurses also spent a lot of time reassuring them that it was okay to fly.

That fall, we were sent to a staging area in England where we got ready to cross the English Channel and support the troops fighting in France. Until then, we wore nurses' seersucker uniforms, but once we arrived in France, we wore combat military uniforms just like the men—wool slacks, a wool shirt, combat boots—and that became our uniform the remainder of the war.

Lunch from mess kits at Camp Crowder, Missouri, June, 1944

From October 1944 until the end of the war, we were on the front lines in the European Theater in France, and then Germany. We would take care of the wounded when they were brought into the hospital—often straight from the battlefield—prepare them for surgery, and tend them afterwards. After a brief recovery period of three or four days, we sent them to a hospital further back from the line, and our hospital would move forward to stay near the battle lines. If a soldier was bleeding severely or suffered some other life-threatening problem, he had to be taken care of immediately—that's why we were there right behind the front lines. We saw absolutely every type of wound—stomach wounds, head wounds and amputations.

Of course, we always checked for frostbite, trench foot and other cold-related injuries since the snowy winter of 1944 was one of the coldest in that part of Europe in half a century. Cold-related injuries are preventable, to some extent, by keeping your feet dry, and General Patton was very firm that the men do the best they could. He ordered them to carry dry socks and change them every day. They carried the socks either under their armpits, or in their crotch, where they would stay dry.

Our hospital moved forty times from October to the following April when we left for Germany. We went where we were needed most. Occasionally we would arrive at a place that had been designated as our hospital, and there would be men on litters waiting for us.

Sometimes the hospital was set up in tents, or, if possible, we might be given a school. Schools made good hospitals because the large rooms could be used for wards, and the smaller ones for operating rooms and nurses quarters. Otherwise we all slept in tents.

COURTESY OF DOROTHY DAVIS

Doing laundry near enemy lines in France, 1944

When the wounded saw the nurses, they would say things like, "Gee, if they're sending women this close to the front, it can't be that bad." We laughed about that later—we were actually so close to the front that we could hear the bombing. Our hospital was bombed several times, in fact. Once, we were in Sarrebourg, a little village in France, when enemy planes hit part of our hospital. I was lined up in the chow line for lunch, and my mess kit went one way, and I went another. None of the patients or staff was injured, but a number of people from the village were—many came to our hospital for treatment. Even though we weren't there to take care of civilians, we managed to provide the necessary first aid, and get them to a hospital in one of the larger towns.

Ours was not the only hospital bombed. There were nineteen nurses killed from enemy action, and more than two hundred nurses died during the war. Most of those that were killed from enemy action died when their hospitals were bombed.

We often had to get out in a hurry because the Germans were advancing, and on several occasions we didn't have enough vehicles to transport all of us. It was always difficult to prepare the patients—who had just undergone surgery—for a long ride over bumpy roads that had been shelled.

We often had to move in the middle of the night during blackout conditions over snowy, icy roads, so the tanks and the troops could use the roads during the daytime. This made for some very long days—I think we all suffered from sleep deprivation. People sometimes ask, "How long did you work?" We worked until the patients were taken care of. When there were only five of us nurses, we really didn't have any choice. We would try to arrange our schedules so that when someone was sleeping, someone else was on duty.

During the Battle of the Bulge, we went a month without a shower. It was too cold for an outdoor shower, so we just took little sponge baths out of our helmets—it's amazing how you could manage. Despite the hardships, we always tried to make ourselves look as presentable as possible. For example, we wore lipstick—it was sort of a morale booster. The guys would wake up from surgery and here was a woman with lipstick on—it meant a lot to them. And now, years later, when I talk to these men, they say, "You know, to wake up and have that nurse there was like seeing an angel of mercy." Psychologically, our presence and "hand-holding" was almost as important as our technical skills.

The 57th was not officially assigned to the Battle of the Bulge, but we were based in the Alsace area of France, in the Vosges Mountains bordering Belgium. We took care of many of the wounded from that forty-day battle, which began December 16, 1944, and ended January 25, 1945. There were more than eighty thousand casualties, including nineteen thousand killed. We later learned that during one week of the

Bulge, our hospital cared for the wounded from twenty-four battalions of troops. We treated troops from other nations, too, that were fighting in the same area with the Americans. If they were wounded, we took care of them.

To constantly be around so much death and misery was not easy—after all, I was only twenty-one. But I felt I had a purpose there, to be part of the war effort, and it was imperative that I not let my emotions take over. I had to keep my wits about me in order to care for the wounded. Everybody was afraid, and everybody had concerns, but if fear took over, then you were unable to do your job. I really tried to keep in mind that this was a job that was absolutely essential.

The 57th Field Hospital continued to follow the U.S. Army through France and into Germany in the spring of 1945. In April, as the war came to a close, Davis and her detachment were based in Germany, where they took care of men wounded from mines and other accidents, received some of the first American POWs to be liberated, and helped evacuate wounded GIs to the U.S.

Davis came home on December 14, 1945, seven months after the war ended. The next month, she married Colonel William Davis, the adjutant for the 57th Field Hospital.

She worked in the Veterans' Hospital in Denville, Illinois, briefly, and when her husband, who stayed in the army, was transferred overseas, she became an "army wife," following her husband to his postings, and the mother of three daughters. Regardless of where they were stationed, Japan, France or Germany, Davis remained involved with the local Red Cross, usually through the school health programs that gave immunization shots to children or working on first-aid projects.

When the family returned to the States from their last overseas assignment and settled in the Washington area, Davis volunteered on various projects at Red Cross national headquarters. American Red Cross national headquarters has twice honored her with the Clara Barton Award.

After Davis's husband died in 1979, she became involved with preserving the history of the Battle of the Bulge. She is a charter member of the Veterans of the Battle of the Bulge, and past president of Battle of the Bulge Historical Foundation. She also served as Red Cross national chairwoman of the observances of the fiftieth anniversary of World War II in 1995 and the fiftieth anniversary of the Korean War in 2003.

In 2004 Davis was one of the one hundred World War II veterans selected by the French government to travel to France to commemorate the sixtieth anniversary of D-Day. In a ceremony with fifteen heads of state in attendance, Davis and the other veterans were granted France's most prestigious military award, the Legion of Honor.

Ruth Sulzberger Holmberg
Chattanooga, Tennessee

Ruth Sulzberger Holmberg is the daughter of legendary New York Times *publisher Arthur Hays Sulzberger, who ran the paper from 1935 to 1961. After she graduated from Smith College in 1943, she spent more than two years during World War II as a Red Cross volunteer in England and France. When she returned, Holmberg moved to Chattanooga, Tennessee, where she was publisher of the* Chattanooga Times *for some thirty years. The Sulzberger family still owns and runs the* New York Times.

My father was an enormously patriotic person and he couldn't serve in the military because of a disability. He was in his late forties, maybe even in his fifties, and he had a bad heart when World War II broke out.

He encouraged me to go in his place, so when I got out of college that's what I did. I was just twenty-two years old, but you were supposed to be twenty-five to volunteer for the Red Cross. But my father was on the Board of Governors of the Red Cross—I think he pulled a few strings and that's why I got in even though I was officially too young.

Everyone was doing something for the war effort. In those days one didn't argue with the country about

COURTESY OF THE UNIVERSITY OF
TENNESSEE AT CHATTANOOGA
**Ruth Holmberg and her son,
Arthur Golden**

the wisdom of being in a war. It was "our country, right or wrong." And so I was very keen to do my part. It never crossed my mind to do otherwise.

Some made Bundles for Britain filled with scarves and blankets, or knit sweaters to go overseas. Since all of the men were being drafted, jobs at home needed filling. My older sister, Marian, drove an ambulance in New York City as a volunteer.

My mother did all those things, and she used to entertain wounded soldiers from hospitals in the New York area. She would invite them up to our weekend house in White Plains to spend the day, and they would come up in ambulances, on crutches, in wheelchairs and stretchers.

Once I arrived in England, my first assignment was in Chelmsford, just north of London. We were on the route between London and the Continent. The German planes would fly over us first on their way to London, then dump the bombs on us on the way back from London. In Chelmsford we were stationed at an airfield that the engineers were still building, and so our job was to make preparations for the Red Cross club being built. Our headquarters for the time being was a tiny tent that subsequently became the post office.

The 394th Bomb Crew, a medium-sized air force bomb crew, moved into the field when it was completed. It was 1943, two years before the war ended. There were two of us there, as always, and we did the usual thing, coffee and donuts. We would go out to the field and serve coffee and donuts when the boys were going to fly missions and we were there when they returned. It was so cold, and scary, because they were going off, and we never knew how many planes or men were coming back. The worst part of it all was that these were people we *knew*.

After they took off, we would go back to the club and wait, and then we'd go back out to the field as they came back and count the planes. When you know people whose plane doesn't come back, you have to assume that they are dead, not that they're prisoners. Of course, I never really knew what had happened to most of the men. They were even younger than I was. It was just awful, but you learned to accept it.

I was attached to the 394th Bomb Crew, so when they moved,

I moved. After we left Chelmsford, we were sent to Saint Lô, in Normandy, the focus of the Normandy invasion in 1944, where we opened up a Red Cross club in some tents. We went from there to Cambrai, which is further east, above Paris, where we had a very big club, in an old restaurant in the town. Next, we ended up on the Holland-German border.

But serving coffee and donuts was not our principal occupation. I was a club director when we got to the Continent. The club was a refuge for enlisted men, not for officers. When they had time off, they'd come to the club. We played games—cribbage and checkers, that kind of thing—and we'd put on dances and shows for them. We would write letters for them—some soldiers were totally illiterate—sew on their buttons, and always be a shoulder to weep on. We were alternative girlfriends or mothers or whatever. We always wore uniforms—they were *hideous*. A skirt and military blouse, sensible shoes and stockings. The skirt was well below the knee, way down low. And we wore helmets out in the field.

It's easy for people to say that we were all over there sleeping with the troops. Nobody ever accused me of that directly, but that's not an original thought—they'll say that about any group of women in a minority with a bunch of men. But we were perfectly normal, hardworking people. We weren't there to pick up a husband, although I admit I did.

His name was Ben Golden, and he was a lieutenant in the bomb crew. He was a ground officer, not a pilot. Before the war, he worked for the Tennessee Valley Authority in Knoxville, Tennessee. We met when the group came in on the field—he was one of the first people I met.

I was overseas just over two years. I remember my father saying that as long as there are servicemen there, you should be there. I didn't quite agree with that. I was ready to come home after two years and I was still there. Peace was declared on May 7th, 1945, but our jobs really didn't change. There was no bombing, but the troops were still there. So we continued doing whatever we could, writing letters, cheering people up, providing entertainment. I came home a couple of months after that, in the fall of '45.

I remember my homecoming vividly. As we pulled into Boston Harbor on a troop ship we were watching a little boat, the port commander's launch, with a man on it who was looking through binoculars at us. I said to the person next to me, "I know this sounds crazy, but that looks like my father." Then this sign unfurled, "Hi Ruthie," and everyone on the ship started chanting, "Hi Ruthie! Who's Ruthie?!" This poor Ruthie nearly fell overboard.

I was told to go to the port commander's office when I got off the ship. I had a little dog I had picked up in Germany—Ben had found him and given him to me. It was a wirehaired dachshund—he was incredibly cute. My name is Ruth and Ben's name is Ben, so we named him Ruben.

I walked into the commander's office with this dog in my knapsack, and my father was standing there. I dropped my knapsack to wrap myself around my father's neck and this dog crawled out. "How did you get the dog on?" the commander asked me. "Oh," I said. "Sailors smuggled it on for me." Just what the commander wanted to hear! He had just finished talking with my father about an influx of pets that was come back from Europe with the troops. And my father had given him this great advice—I don't remember what it was, but he certainly wasn't recommending that they let them all in—and then I came in with this dog. My father was so mad at me—I thought my father was gonna kill me! Luckily, he let me keep the dog.

In June 1946, eight months after returning to the States, Ruth Sulzberger married Ben Golden in White Plains, New York. The couple went to live in Knoxville, Tennessee, but a few months later, Arthur Sulzberger offered his new son-in-law a job working for the Times-*owned Chattanooga* Times, *and he soon became publisher. The couple had four children: Stephen Golden, an attorney in Arizona, Michael Golden, publisher of the* International Herald Tribune *and vice chairman of the* New York Times, *Lynn Dolnick, associate director of the National Zoo in Washington, D.C., and Arthur Golden, an author who wrote the best-selling novel,* Memories of a Geisha. *Holmberg has seven grandchildren.*

When the couple divorced, Ruth Sulzberger took over the position of publisher of the Chattanooga Times. *In 1972 Ruth Sulzberger married William Holmberg, circulation manager of the* New York Times. *He passed away in 2005.*

In the summer of 2003, Ruth Holmberg, age 82, opened a drawer full of letters written to her father that she had stashed away after the war. She hadn't read them in more than fifty years. "I was really bothered about people talking about their war experiences constantly and bragging about how brave they were and how close to death they came," she recalls, "and I swore up and down that I'd never discuss it—and I didn't—until now."

Mary Minamoto
Portland, Oregon

In the spring of 1942, Mary Minamoto and her family were among the more than one hundred thousand people of Japanese ancestry forced to leave their homes—in what amounted to the largest forced relocation in U.S. history. Minamoto's family was sent to the Minidoka War Relocation Center, a huge camp in south-central Idaho that housed nearly ten thousand Japanese Americans at its peak in 1943.

Minamoto was allowed to leave the camp to attend college in Salt Lake City, Utah, while the war was still on. Two of her younger brothers also left the camp—they volunteered to fight the war for the Allies. A third brother later served in the Korean War.

When she graduated from college in 1945, Minamoto returned to Portland, where she took a job with the American Red Cross. It was a natural fit—her mother was a Red Cross volunteer who hosted fundraising events before the war. "Once, she hosted a costume show with traditional Japanese clothing, including my mother's wedding kimono," recalls Minamoto.

She worked for the American Red Cross for thirty-six years before her retirement in 1979.

War broke out December 7, 1941. We had to evacuate from our home on May 20, 1942. I was twenty-one years old.

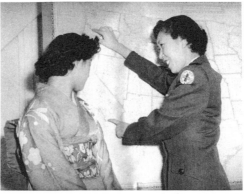

COURTESY OF THE AMERICAN RED CROSS

Mary Minamoto, Japan, 1955

My folks were raising strawberries—we had a hundred acres of strawberries. Our farm was a sharecrop. The berries were already ripe and ready for harvesting, but we were told, "You folks can't stay—you have to go to an internment camp." So the berries went bad at harvest that year.

We were told we could only take one suitcase for the whole family. They told us what we could take—basically just clothes. We had to leave everything else behind.

Before we went to the camp, there were rumors that we were going to be sent to Japan. We said, "What the heck are we going to do in Japan? We don't know their customs or anything." I was born and grew up in Olympia, Washington. Both of my parents were born in Japan, but they spoke English. Our parents told us, "You're American—this is your country." My brothers and sisters and I were born here. Yet they treated us like foreigners.

We were evacuated from our home to the Pacific Livestock Exposition on the outskirts of Portland, Oregon. There we slept in horses' stalls, with that smell, that stench—I can still remember it. We were given army cots with straw mattresses to sleep on. We had no doors—there were just two big canvas curtains hanging. Overhead, it was all glass windows—I think the FBI was walking around watching. We had a curfew—even adults had to be indoors at 8:00 P.M. They would come around with a flashlight to make sure we were all in bed.

Three and a half months later, on September 3, 1942—I remember the date exactly—we were put on a rickety train, with the shades all down, and we were sent to the Minidoka War Relocation Center in Idaho. We lived in army barracks and we had nothing but potbelly stoves to keep us warm. There were lots of dust storms. It was nothing but scorpions and sagebrush—when the wind blew, sand crept in the cracks around the windows.

At the camp, I worked as a teacher's assistant for fifth grade students. In eastern Idaho, they had potatoes and onions, but they had no one to harvest crops because the Caucasians were being drafted into service, so the men and boys from the camp, including my father and brothers, worked as farmhands. Later, the boys, Harry and Ned, said, "We will prove we are Americans by serving our country." They volunteered and went into military service and got sent overseas to the battlefields in Europe and the Far East. My mother and my youngest brother and sister stayed at the camp until it closed in July of 1945.

We didn't know how long they would keep us and I just wanted to get out of camp as soon as I could. I wanted to hurry and learn something fast, because 1 was not prepared to work—I had only worked in the field to help my parents after school. Besides, we had no indication that we would ever be able to return to our home.

We had to get FBI clearance to go to school. It took quite a while for me to get it—eight months. Finally, in May of 1943, I took a Greyhound bus to Utah to go to Henager Business College in Salt Lake City.

Once I arrived, the principal sent me to the Japanese-American Citizens League. He wanted to reassure me there was nothing to be scared of, but I had no fear of white people. We had lived in Olympia, a mainstream community. To me, living among Caucasians was nothing out of the ordinary, but his sending me there turned out to be my good fortune, because the Japanese-American League was located across the hall from the Red Cross. I was coming and going and, in time, I got to know the people at the Red Cross, and they asked me to volunteer. But I needed money because I was determined to go to college, so I was working, both for an attorney, as well as babysitting and taking odd jobs. I needed to earn money for tuition and room and board.

In 1945 I returned to Portland when the military curfew against Japanese Americans was lifted. I had been in touch with the War Relocation Authority director in Portland, and his wife was a Red Cross volunteer. The Red Cross manager started calling me. He was also a Methodist minister and we were a Methodist family—that's how he knew me. He called me every day for three days in a row and said, "Come to Red Cross." I thought he was looking for volunteers, so I kept saying, "Sorry, 1 can't come today because I need to find a job before I can do any volunteer work." He said he had a job for me—a paying job—and so I finally went in to talk to him about working at the Red Cross.

My first job was as a receptionist and teletypist for the Portland chapter. We handled emergencies from the surrounding areas within a hundred-mile radius of Portland. When there was a problem back home or a death in the family, the Red Cross social workers would call the family doctor to get a diagnosis and ask whether the serviceman needed to come home. When we got an answer from the doctor, I would send a teletype to the Red Cross installation overseas.

I worked nights at first. The social workers would have telegrams stacked up for me when I came on duty at 4:00 P.M. to send to Red Cross chapters throughout the U.S. and overseas. Portland was the district headquarters so wires were coming and going all of the time.

In time, I became a volunteer anyway, as an interpreter for the Japanese War Brides School, which had been set up to teach Japanese girls who had married U.S. soldiers about American customs. When the boys had to go back overseas, or to an installation in the Midwest or on the East Coast, some of the Japanese girls who had married them got stranded here without family. The girls could hardly understand the language, or the western customs, and many of them had a hard time. In Japan, the custom was that the first wife had the children, the second wife took care of the books, and the third wife was a social companion. In the War Brides School, we taught them that in America, the wife manages the home and also takes care of the budget—she also has the children, of course, and is the companion as well.

COURTESY OF THE AMERICAN RED CROSS
War Brides School, Yokohama, Japan

Another Japanese custom is for families to send girls off to cooking and sewing schools before they marry, but since some of them had run away to marry their American sweethearts, this didn't happen. Some were totally unprepared to be American wives and mothers. We taught them that a certain day was washday, and the next day was ironing day, and another day was grocery-shopping day. They were taught how to serve tea and be a good hostess. In addition, army nurses would tell them about hygiene, and how to care for their children.

In September 1953, I was asked to transfer to Japan. I was the first "Nisei"—American born of Japanese ancestry—to be sent abroad anywhere by the Red Cross. I had various jobs there. Once again, I worked as an interpreter for the War Brides School, but this time in Japan, for the wives whose servicemen-husbands had already gone to the U.S. The brides I taught would be following them later. I also accompanied field directors on home visits to Japanese brides to make arrangements for the girls to go to the U.S.

In 1956 I came back home to the Portland chapter and worked in the personnel department until 1971, when I was again transferred, this time to the Pacific Area headquarters in San Francisco. There I worked as a staff assistant in the personnel office until I retired in 1979.

Minamoto moved back to Portland, where she took a part-time job organizing programs and activities for the local YWCA. She also taught Ikebana, Japanese flower arranging, which she learned while she was living in Japan, at the Woodstock Community Center.

Minamoto volunteers as a board member of the Osteoporosis Support Group of Providence Portland Medical Center. She relies on a Red Cross van to transport her to water-therapy classes three times a week.

Both of Mary Minamoto's brothers who served in WWII, and her brother who served in the Korean War, returned safely from combat.

Josephine "Jo" Sippy Schwaebe
Del Mar, California

By the time the U.S. entered the war in 1941, Jo Sippy Schwaebe, a twenty-three year old airline hostess based in Washington, D.C., knew many people fighting in World War II one way or another. "Everybody who was anybody came to Washington, so we had many people on the flights who were important to the war effort," says Schwaebe, who worked for a regional carrier.

Schwaebe decided to make a career change one night while on a layover in Detroit. She was eating dinner in a pub with fellow crewmembers when the jukebox played George M. Cohan's famous war song, Over There. *"I was so stirred by the music, I had to do something," recalls Schwaebe. She returned to Washington, and applied for an overseas position with the American Red Cross.*

When Schwaebe arrived in London on December 29, 1942, she landed a coveted job at the newly opened Rainbow Corner, the famous Red Cross club near Piccadilly Square. Schwaebe, who was known as "Sippy" during the year and a half she worked at the club, was one of a handful of American Red Cross girls amidst thousands of British volunteers and staff.

Rainbow Corner was open twenty four hours a day from November 11, 1942, until January 9, 1946. The club was the hub of wartime recreation in London for thousands of GIs

COURTESY OF JO SCHWAEBE

preparing for the D-Day invasion, and later became a respite for GIs on leave. In July of 1943, soldiers visited the place 331,709 times, and by December, the number of entries for the month increased to 572,036. On average, the club served forty thousand meals a day. "The place was a beehive of activity," recalls Schwaebe. "There was something for everyone in that club, from chamber music to boxing matches."

Rainbow Corner had been open about a month when Harvey Gibson, head of the Red Cross in England, put me there. Actually, the staff was hand-picked—and if you didn't work out, you didn't stay.

Gibson's wife, Helen, really ran the place. She was gentle and she was fair—she was a lovely, kind woman, very pretty and regal. She added an aura to the place that was quite elegant. She'd buy cameras with her personal money and lend them to the boys who didn't have one. She would say to them, "Take it for the day and bring it back with you." If a GI was disappointed about not getting a ticket to something, she'd manage to get one with her own money.

COURTESY OF JO SCHWAEBE

What made Rainbow Corner unique was the location. The area around Piccadilly Square was wild, and it was blackout time, of course. You couldn't walk through the neighborhood without hearing "How much for all night?" Harvey Gibson wanted a place where the guys could go to get off the street, and the GIs wanted someplace they could take refuge. Rainbow Corner wasn't a place to sleep—just a place to come, rest, shower and eat. Actually, the meals weren't so hot, but the guys came in droves.

Hans Crescent, another Red Cross club in London, was a very nice club and they had lovely girls working there, but it had a totally different, calmer atmosphere. At Rainbow Corner, we were kind of—I don't want to say "wild," but it was a fun place, and it was noisy. We had a lot of action.

At the club, the GIs could get all kinds of information—volunteers answered questions about transportation, where to shop, what to buy, and what to see in the city. The Red Cross field director—a go-between for emergencies back home—had a desk in the lobby, and there was a soda fountain to give the place some hometown atmosphere.

The dining room was on the second level, and off of that we had this huge amusement room, where the GIs could play games like pinball or listen to the jukebox. Upstairs on the third floor there was a huge room with a stage where we held boxing matches, parties and stage shows. We had a lot of British people like Bea Lillie come in and entertain the guys. We also held the dances there. Dance hostesses—British girls who came to dance with the guys—were screened before being allowed in. Most of them were really nice. They just wanted a good time and to meet a guy—their men were all gone. Girls were ushered in and brought right up to the dance hall, and then they would meet someone and dance. The hookers wanted to come in too, but the club would try to keep as many out as possible. Of course, there were some naughty things going on, but by and large most people came to dance and have fun.

On the third floor there was a little room where Gibson and his wife entertained special guests with food and cocktails. General Eisenhower, Winston Churchill, the Harrimans, the actress Bebe Daniels, Count

Bernadotte, the head of the Swedish Red Cross, and Jimmy Stewart—they all dropped in. Anybody who was anybody came. Irving Berlin was a personal friend of Mrs. Gibson's—he came several times. I was always asked to help out there, and those of us who did got to know most of these people quite well because of these little parties.

Above the dance hall was a large room with a piano, tables and chairs for writing letters or playing cards, and comfortable chairs for reading and relaxing. Harold Bowler, who did the World War II painting of a pair of tired GI shoes that's hanging in the Smithsonian, taught painting classes to the soldiers up there. There was also a music room, where a girl named Judy played the piano. We also had chamber music and concerts.

Downstairs in the basement, we had the "American Eagle," a radio show, broadcast to America and I helped select the boys who were on the program. They were asked questions on the air like where they were from and whether they wanted to say hello to someone back home. Once a week, the Glenn Miller Band came and played too. Another regular downstairs was Lady Adele "Dellie" Astaire—Fred Astaire's sister—who was there every day writing letters home for the boys. Mrs. Whitaker, a volunteer, darned socks and sewed buttons and insignias on the boys' uniforms.

COURTESY OF JO SCHWAEBE

The American Eagle radio program broadcast to America from Rainbow Corner

There was also a large area downstairs that served as a place for the boys to go and relax and chitchat. There were tables and chairs, a donut and coffee bar, fortune-tellers and a jukebox—the room was noisy and fun. I worked all over the club, but primarily, I was down there floating around and talking to the soldiers—lending an ear was very important.

When I arrived in England, there weren't a lot of Americans there yet. Many of the boys who came to the Red Cross were around my age—twenty-three—so in essence I was kind of the girl next door, and a reminder of home. Mostly the conversations were light—I asked them things like, "Where are you from? Where did you go to school, or did you know so and so?"

As time went by the boys became more lonely. The conversations became more meaningful. For example, we would discuss family problems, or illnesses, or the Dear John letters they had received. The airmen were particularly open with their feelings. They worried about their next mission and were haunted by seeing their friends' planes shot down. Sometimes they would call me from an air base to tell of a lost soldier. Sometimes I received letters from POWs who remembered me from Rainbow Corner, and I would write back. The correspondence was light and not detailed, as their outgoing and incoming mail was censored.

We also had a first-aid room—it was mostly where we let the drunks sober up. We would bring them in if we saw a drunk GI on the street or the MPs would bring them in, and we'd sort of lock them up until they sobered up. We took care of them and gave them food, so they were well enough to get on the train and go back to their base. Most of the guys had just come to London for a good time, and some had *too* good a time.

By 1944 England was jam-packed with Americans. The club was crowded and busy and things were less personal. Just before the invasion of Europe, some of the GIs were pretty troubled. The guys knew that an invasion was imminent and they were worried. It was scary for us all—they were younger than I was, and I was young!

Shortly after the D-Day invasion, many paratroopers came back and many did not. Some shared their first encounters with war—what it was like to see so much killing and seeing their buddies hanging from trees by their head and feet. After the invasion, most of the guys were gone or lost, but some of them came back on leave. Some of them came back terribly tattered, torn and burned.

One particular incident will always remain with me. One day some airmen, who had survived airplane crashes while flying missions and were patients at a nearby hospital, came into Rainbow Corner. One boy said to me, "Hey Jo, remember me?" Of course, I said yes, and took his hand, which had been badly burned. His face was burned too and his eyelids and nose—Oh God, I can't really describe how awful it was. We talked about him having a complete recovery. The entire time was challenging, demanding and exciting. I feel privileged to have served my country as a Red Cross worker, and to have been a part of so many taxing and difficult circumstances experienced by our military personnel.

Jo Schwaebe was sent to France in August 1944, where she worked in various makeshift clubs in places like Normandy and Versailles. After Paris was liberated on August 25, 1944, Schwaebe was transferred to a Red Cross club in Paris, also called Rainbow Corner, which was housed in the Hotel de Paris.

In December Schwaebe returned to her hometown, St. Louis, because her father was ill. She worked on a war fund drive for a couple of months, raising money for the Red Cross by speaking at local meetings. She went back to Paris in the spring and stayed at Rainbow Corner until June 1945.

After the war, Schwaebe was awarded the Bronze Star. She married Harry Schwaebe, an air force pilot who was in the Army of Occupation. The couple spent two years in Japan, where two of Schwaebe's five children were born. She eventually divorced her husband and settled in San Diego, where she began a career in social work, which she had studied at Washington University in St. Louis. She retired in 1982.

Chapter 2

MORE THAN COFFEE AND DONUTS

When I was a young man, I thought glory was the highest ambition, and that all glory was self-glory. My parents tried to teach me otherwise, as did the Naval Academy. But I didn't understand the lesson until later in life, when I confronted challenges I never expected to face. In that confrontation, I discovered that I was dependent on others to a greater extent than I had ever realized, but that neither they nor the cause we served made any claims on my identity. On the contrary, they gave me a larger sense of myself than I had before. And I am a better man for it. I discovered that nothing is more liberating than to fight for a cause larger than yourself; something that encompasses you, but is not defined by your existence alone. I honor all of you who have devoted yourself to this noble organization. You are providing an example to our children that is an antidote for the selfishness of our times. You are helping them to discover that while the vanities of youth prove ephemeral, something better can endure, and endure until our last moment on earth. And that is the love we give and the honor we earn when we sacrifice with others for something greater than our self-interest.

— Senator John McCain (R-Arizona), in a 1999 speech at the American Red Cross Humanity conference

S ince Clara Barton's heroic actions caring for wounded soldiers on the fields of the Civil War earned her the name, the Angel of the Battlefield, the American Red Cross has continued a unique partnership with the military. Regardless of the type of conflict or where it occurs in the world, the Red Cross serves as the chief means of communication between the military and their families back home. On the eve of Operation Iraqi Freedom in 2003 former Red Cross President Senator Elizabeth Dole told Congress: "Many people do not realize that wherever our military goes, the Red Cross goes with them to provide support and services, delivering approximately four thousand emergency messages a day to our men and women."

American Red Cross personnel have supported every major international conflict or humanitarian crisis throughout its 125-year history. During the Korean Conflict in the 1950s, Red Cross field directors were stationed on bases to help troops with family and personal problems. After Harry Truman designated the Red Cross as the blood collecting agency for the nation's military in 1951, it sent five million pints of blood to Korea. Supplemental Recreational Activities Overseas (SRAO) workers, teams of young women called "Donut Dollies," were sent to entertain and boost the morale of the troops in Korea. Lucie Davidson, who spent two years in that capacity, refers to the job as "the greatest experience of my life"—a sentiment she estimates is shared by ninety percent of her peers. "It was exciting, interesting and a real education," says Davidson, who still attends Donut Dollie reunions. "Friends made then are still friends today."

The American Red Cross was called into action several times throughout the Cold War. After the failed Bay of Pigs invasion in 1962, the agency helped negotiate the release of 751 Cuban prisoners and their families, and brought them to the U.S. A banana boat emblazoned with a large red cross dropped off millions of dollars in medical supplies and food in Havana, then ferried passengers to Fort Lauderdale with a U.S. Coast Guard escort. Roy Popkin, who helped secure the refugees' release, recalls what it was like being there during the evacuation: "The first lady who climbed the gangplank fell to her knees and made the sign of the cross when she saw the American flag hanging from the fantail of the ship."

At the height of the Vietnam War in the late 1960s, the Red Cross had five hundred staff stationed in that war-torn country. Two million emergency communications were transmitted between servicemen stationed in Indochina and their families. General William Westmoreland, commander of U.S. forces in Southeast Asia, wrote to the Red Cross in 1968 stating: "Serving our men on the battlefields here in Vietnam, the American Red Cross is a hotline to the folks back home, an oasis in the heat of battle, and a comfort during hospitalization."

John Cataldo is one of the people who Westmoreland was writing about. He spent thirty-two years with the Red Cross, including nearly two decades overseas, assigned to bases in Turkey, Germany, Korea and Vietnam, where he was awarded the Purple Heart when his hut was blown up.

COURTESY OF THE AMERICAN RED CROSS
Red Cross mercy ship bound for Cuba, 1963

The mainstay of Cataldo's job for many of those years was to facilitate emergency leave for servicemen and women. "A young man would come to me and say, 'My father died and I have to go home and run the family farm,'" remembers Cataldo. "We would help the young man document what was needed to process that kind of a discharge."

For Vietnam veterans, the more than seven hundred women who cheered them up during that bloody conflict will always remain the face of the Red Cross. When the National Vietnam Veterans Memorial in Washington, D.C. was dedicated in 1982 the Donut Dollies had a float on a flatbed truck. Veterans kept running up to the women on the float and hugging them and thanking them for being in Vietnam with them. "Without Donut Dollies in Vietnam, it would have been much harder for all of us that served there," reads a posting on a Donut Dollie Web site. "You and others like you made it a better place to be."

Of course, the Red Cross was also involved in other wartime activities. As the conflict came to an end, the Red Cross provided assistance to thousands of Vietnamese refugees, and it played a vital role in what was known as Operation Babylift, bringing nearly two thousand Vietnamese orphans to the U.S.

Although the Red Cross no longer has a program to entertain troops, staffers continue to play a role in overseas conflicts and on peacekeeping operations. During Operation Desert Shield and Desert Storm in 1990, 158 Armed Forces Emergency Services (AFES) staff members were stationed in the Persian Gulf region. Since then, AFES staff have been deployed to Somalia, Rwanda, Haiti, Croatia, Bosnia and Kosovo, to name a few.

Operation Iraqi Freedom is no exception. Some two hundred staff have served in Kuwait and Iraq since 2003—the largest deployment of personnel since Operation Desert Storm. Their main job is relaying emergency messages between troops and their families in the U.S. Even though e-mail and cell phones often make communicating between GIs and their loved ones easier, it's not always possible. "When the troops are in the field, they don't have access to the new technology, but we have access to them," explains Philip Chapman, a volunteer and former Red Cross field manager in Vietnam and elsewhere. "Red Cross staff provide a certain peace of mind for the person back home and the serviceperson." More importantly, the Red Cross will track down a doctor or a funeral home director to verify an illness or a death so that the military will grant an emergency leave to the soldier. "We've come to be highly respected and trusted by the military commanders." explains Wendy Dyer, senior Red Cross station manager at Fort Bragg, North Carolina.

Dyer was stationed in Iraq in 2004. She and three other Red Cross workers lived and worked in trailers on Victory Base in Baghdad. They braved 100-degree heat, and endured bombs and rockets going off day and night. "One night a bomb hit so close it blew the trailer door open while we were delivering Red Cross messages," she recalls. "We slept with our flak vest, boots and Kevlar within reach, and we learned to roll of bed and hit the floor fast." The team also had to use unreliable communications systems. "There were times when we were inundated with Red Cross messages—we received about fifty on a twelve-hour shift and there were many shifts where we had one hundred messages."

When a large number of national guardsmen were activated for military duty after the first Gulf War, the Red Cross instituted the "Get to know us before you need us" program, designed to let local guardsmen and their families learn what services the agency offers in times of emergency. Sue Richter, vice president for AFES for more than a decade before she retired in 2005, explains that the success of this outreach had transformed local chapters into "the point of contact not only in times of emergency, but year round."

Red Cross chapters also assisted the families of military personnel stateside, particularly helpful today since so many assignments in Iraq have been extended. Numerous chapters offer support groups for family members of overseas soldiers, and several have their own morale-boosting efforts. The Greater Carolina chapter in Charlotte collects "sacks-o-smiles" for servicemen overseas filled with novels, lip balms, sunscreen lotions, and snacks. The Ottawa County chapter in Holland, Michigan, sends phone cards to make free calls back home. The American people are so generous," recalls Dyer, who has been deployed to Germany, Hungary and Kosovo during her seventeen-year Red Cross career. "They would send cameras, alarm clocks with Tweety bird sounds—anything to put a smile on a service member's face."

International health programs are another facet of the American Red Cross. One example is the Measles Initiative, a five-year plan to eradicate measles in African children. Launched in 2001 in conjunction with the U.S. Centers for Disease Control and Prevention (CDC) and the United Nations Foundation, the program has vaccinated more than 111 million children.

In recent years the organization has stepped up its role aiding foreign countries in the aftermath of large calamities. For example, American Red Cross personnel were sent to Central America in 1998 after Hurricane Mitch and to Izmit, Turkey, after the 1999 earthquake. Most recently, staffers were dispatched to the scene of the deadly tsunami that struck Asia on December 26, 2004, killing nearly 200,000 people from twelve countries.

The American Red Cross is also an affiliate of the International Committee of the Red Cross (ICRC), a neutral body whose mission is to uphold the Geneva Conventions protecting the rights of victims of war during armed conflicts. After the abuses at the infamous Abu Ghraib prison in Iraq became public in 2004, the relevance of the ICRC and the Geneva Conventions came under question. Senator John McCain, who has publicly credited the Geneva Conventions for ensuring that he was more or less treated humanely while he

COURTESY OF RICARDO CAIVANO

Relief distribution line, Sri Lanka, 2005

was a POW in Vietnam, has defended the ICRC. In a 2004 column in the *Wall Street Journal*, he wrote: "It is critical to realize that the Red Cross and the Geneva conventions do not endanger American soldiers, they protect them. Our soldiers enter battle with the knowledge that should they be taken prisoner there are laws intended to protect them and impartial international observers to inquire after them."

Sharon Vander Ven Cummings
Pasadena, California

Four months after receiving her college diploma in 1966, Sharon Vander Ven signed up for a year as a Donut Dollie in Vietnam. When she was a child, her family lived overseas because her father was in the military and the American Red Cross's Supplemental Recreational Activities Overseas (SRAO) program sounded like an exciting opportunity—certainly better than a nine-to-five job.

When she arrived in Vietnam, Cummings was just a few months past her twenty-first birthday—the youngest Donut Dollie in the country at the time. Nearly forty years later, she is a technical writer and editor in California, but she still considers her year-long stint in Vietnam the most rewarding experience of her life.

M y father was a pilot in the air force for twenty years. He joined the Army Air Corps straight out of high school in 1943, and flew over Europe during World War II. While we were stationed at Clark Air Force Base in the Philippines from 1952 to 1955, my mother volunteered with the Gray Ladies, and continued with the Red Cross when we were transferred to Barksdale Air Force Base in Louisiana. After my father retired in 1963, Mom took a paying job with the Red Cross in San Bernardino, California. She was still working there when she died in 1978.

COURTESY OF SHARON CUMMINGS

My mother was the one who told me about the SRAO program starting up in Vietnam. You had to be female, at least twenty-one, single, with a college degree. I had just graduated from the University of California, Santa Barbara and I fit all the requirements, so I volunteered to go. The pay was low, but I didn't take the job for the money—I took it for what I could do to help our guys, and for the experience, the excitement and the challenge. Our tour of duty was one year, same as the guys.

I flew to San Francisco for an interview and was offered the job on the spot. Within six weeks, I had gotten some of my shots—for yellow fever, malaria, smallpox and gamma globulin to protect against hepatitis—and was in Washington, D.C. for two weeks of training.

Our training consisted of learning how to recognize the various branches of the military and their ranks, how to behave like a lady in all situations, and a brief tutorial on the responsibilities of our job. We received the rest of our shots at the Pentagon, and we were issued our dog tags and uniforms. Our basic uniform was a powder blue-and-white pin-stripe dress or culottes with black penny loafers, which later was changed to light blue sneakers. For Sunday coffee call and special command appearances, we wore a two-piece suit—a skirt and a fitted jacket—also in blue-and-white pinstripe, with a small hat, and short heels.

Within weeks after signing up, I was on a plane full of GIs with six other girls—we always called ourselves "girls"—and we were on our way to Vietnam. It was a whole new adventure. Having been raised in the military, I was never concerned for my safety—I just *knew* that the government would not send civilians into harm's way. This was 1966, so there had not been a whole lot in the media yet about the war. I had no idea what I was really volunteering for, but I was excited and anxious to go. I look back and cannot believe how innocent and naive I was. I had been raised as an air force brat, and lived in Germany and the Philippines, but I really had led a sheltered life.

Our job was to set up recreation centers before the USO and Special Services came in, and to plan recreation programs to take out in the field for the guys who could not come into our centers. This was called a clubmobile program—it was a mobile recreation program.

Since the soldiers in the hospitals were unable to participate in our fun and games, we visited the hospitals and handed out activity books with puzzles, riddles, cartoons and jokes that we had written and put together. Or, we went into the wards and spent some time with the wounded soldiers—to bring some joy and distraction into their lives, to boost their morale. Our job was to smile and be bubbly—no matter what the situation. We had to let the guys know that we were not repulsed or shocked at how they looked, no matter how bad their injuries. If we could accept them the way they looked, then maybe things would be okay when they got home. For me, this was a very important part of my job, and extremely rewarding.

My first six months were spent at Cam Ranh Bay, which was a support area run by the army. Many of the guys there had come over to fight, but instead were unloading ships and doing other supply details, and consequently, morale was very low. We staffed the recreation center there seven days a week from early morning to late evening.

Sometimes the day was spent running the recreation center. Other times I'd be in the office constructing props for the next clubmobile

COURTESY OF SHARON CUMMINGS

The Sandpipers, a band made up of Donut Dollies and enlisted men

program to take out in the field, or putting together the books for the hospital. Or, the entire day might be spent traveling from site to site by helicopter or jeep to the various units presenting our clubmobile programs. At the site, we had a warm-up activity to get the guys interested, and then the main activity, usually some type of competition. The best way to describe a program is to think of a game show: We'd have a theme (cards, food, ESP, sports) that several games would be centered around. We'd divide the guys into teams and they would compete for pieces of a puzzle or points. The games were always fun—and even the most hardened guys usually lightened up and joined in the craziness of the moment. The object was to have fun and escape the reality, or boredom, of where they were and what they were doing.

Mostly we worked at the recreation center at the base. It was always bustling. We had tapes sent from the states with the latest music—folk songs from Peter, Paul and Mary and the Limelighters were big at the time. In the evenings there would be guitars strumming, a cutthroat game of hearts, or pinochle tournaments, and there was always someone playing pool.

We served Kool-Aid all the time, and coffee and cake on Sunday mornings. We celebrated birthdays with candles in a cardboard cake because we couldn't just go to the grocery store and buy a real cake or mix. We were always thinking of new activities we could offer— luaus, talent shows, carnivals and pool tournaments. We had Monte Carlo nights with gambling—cards, roulette, dice and Monopoly money to place bets. It was all to keep the guys interested and give them an alternative to drinking at their clubs. Remember, a lot of these guys were only nineteen years old. They needed some clean and safe diversions from what was available in the towns. It was a busy, busy place to be. We tried to have something for everyone—there was *always* something to do. I loved it. And I still miss it.

I really loved to sing, so evenings at the center often turned into impromptu hootenannies. And if I was having so much fun, I thought, why not take this idea and turn it into a clubmobile program, which is how the Sandpipers were born. We put together an actual show and took it on the road, after I got permission from the guys' commanding officers. We even did a performance for several hundred guys at the convalescent hospital at Cam Ranh Air Force Base. We all knew that the Sandpipers were temporary, but it was really hard to break up when the girls in the group—including me—were transferred to new bases. The Sandpipers will always have a very special spot in my heart.

My next assignment was Long Binh, which was east of Saigon. Although we had a center there, we focused more on the clubmobile programs. That's where I really saw the wages of war. I saw it in the looks in the guys' eyes when they came in from the field. It's a blank stare—it goes through and past you. As the months wore on, it got harder and harder to greet the new guys with the same enthusiasm, because I knew many of them would not make it back to the States alive. I was still brave and smiled every day, and when a GI asked in amazement, "Why are you here?" I just beamed that smile and answered, "Because you are here!" But I knew that I might be the last American girl he would ever talk to.

It was an intense year because the job was more than just a job, it was a way of life. You dealt with incoming rounds, bunkers, casualties of war, jeeps, eating chow out of cans, being separated from your families, the lack of permanent relationships and friends, loneliness, the strangeness of a foreign land. The days were long and we worked six days a week, sometimes seven. We didn't punch a time clock. Even when you were not on duty officially, you were still on duty, from the moment you woke up in the morning until you crashed at night.

All our time was spent focused on the guys—sometimes just talking to them for hours and hours, but they were so appreciative of our being there. We all gave a great deal of ourselves. No way around it, the year there was emotionally draining. By the time I was transferred to Cu Chi for my final couple of months, I was exhausted, physically and mentally. We all came home wiped out, but being there drew on all my talents and challenged me in a way that was unique. If you asked me to go again today, I'd do it. Even now—nearly forty years later—I still have dreams about going back because I am needed. And I go.

When I returned to the States, I was a burnt-out case. I needed time to decompress, but I was expected to fit right in, as if I had never been to war. I remember one day in the grocery store, I got really upset over the long aisle of cereal boxes. It seemed like hundreds of different types of cereal, and I couldn't help think that to the people at home, it was more important to choose the correct brand of cereal than to worry about our guys who were being blown to bits on the news every night. Nobody seemed to get it that these guys were really dying and that was real blood they were seeing on television. I got so very, very angry. I felt lost. I didn't know what to do next with my life. I felt as if I was expected to find a husband, have a family, and become the housewife that I had been destined to be, but I didn't even know how to act. I would walk down a street and smile at everyone because that was what was expected of me in Nam. Someone finally pointed out to me that I shouldn't be smiling at everyone—people might get the wrong impression.

COURTESY OF SHARON CUMMINGS

Donut Dollies marching in Washington, D.C. at the dedication of the Vietnam Women's Memorial in 1993.

The letdown back in the States was very hard. I had felt valuable in Nam. For a year, I was required to be artistically creative, to draw on my powers of imagination, to interact with all sorts of people of different ages and stations in life from various backgrounds, and to be resourceful when it came to living and working conditions. But back home, my experience in Nam counted for nothing. I couldn't even find a decent job. The self-confidence I gained there was wiped away. Nothing could compare to the fulfillment I had while working with *my* guys in Vietnam.

All the jobs I've had since pale in comparison to the satisfaction I got out of my job in Nam. There was a real excitement and a real challenge to being a Donut Dollie. I saw the good sides of people. Vietnam made me more appreciative of everything I have and everything our country offers us. I am so very grateful to be an American.

When Sharon Cummings returned to the states in the spring of 1967, she found a job working in the dean's office at the University of California at Berkeley, to be near a graduate student she had been dating before going to Vietnam. When her boyfriend left California for a summer job in another state, two fellow Donut Dollies introduced Cummings to a Vietnam veteran who was stationed at the Presidio in San Francisco. They were married two months later, and moved to Akron, Ohio, her husband's hometown. The couple had two daughters; they are now divorced.

Cummings was a stay-at-home mom for a decade, during which she volunteered as a Red Cross swimming instructor at the local high school. In the early 1990s, Cummings was a consultant for the TV show, "China Beach." Today she lives in Santa Clarita, California, and she does administrative support, technical writing and editing for Parsons Corporation, teaches computer programs, and is involved in community theater as an actor, director and newsletter editor. In 1995 she married another Vietnam veteran.

Claude "Pete" Ashen
San Francisco, California

*I*n *Red Cross circles, Pete Ashen is a renowned storyteller. No wonder—his Red Cross career spans forty-five years and dozens of disaster assignments all over the country. Ashen's first big disaster was an Alaskan earthquake in 1964 that registered 8.6 on the Richter scale, and killed more than half of the 139 people living in the small village of Chenega. Another oft-told tale is about a two-month stint working in 1969 as an ICRC delegate during the Nigerian/Biafran Civil War, when he came down with dengue fever. In 1989 Ashen directed the Red Cross disaster relief operation following the Loma Prieta earthquake in San Francisco.*

As Ashen tells it, he became involved in Red Cross disaster work after serving in two wars (World War II and the Korean Conflict), then dabbling at several jobs, including a stint as a sewing-machine salesman and repairman. He was working as an insurance agent for John Hancock Life Insurance Company in 1960, and because he was active in political circles, he was appointed to a citywide disaster council that worked on earthquake preparedness. At a meeting with representatives from the local Red Cross, he challenged them to produce the names of people who would staff a shelter in the event of an earthquake. They became defensive—and then invited him to become a volunteer. "The next thing I knew, I was disaster chairman for the Golden Gate chapter," recalls Ashen.

Six years later Ashen switched from volunteer to paid staff. He served as disaster director in San Francisco for twenty years, and later in his career, was promoted to emergency services manager. Sometimes his job didn't fall under the usual disaster umbrella, and these assignments resulted in his most memorable stories. That was the case in the spring of 1975, just weeks before American forces withdrew from Vietnam. Ashen directed what came to be known as Operation Babylift, the evacuation of thousands of children from Vietnamese orphanages to the U.S.

Over a five-week period, 1,318 babies came through San Francisco alone. Los Angeles and Seattle also acted as way stations for the children before they were sent to adoption agencies all over the country. On a moment's notice, hundreds of Red Cross volunteers were mobilized to help care for the babies around the clock. "It was one of those things where the Red Cross became involved with something that grew out of nowhere," recalls Ashen. "It was just a wonderful outpouring of Red Cross spirit."

In April 1975, just when they thought that the South Vietnamese government was about to fall, a lot of babies were in orphanages there. Many of them were half-Vietnamese and half-black or Caucasian, the children of American GIs. What was terrifying was that the North Vietnamese might massacre all of these children once their troops occupied Saigon, so a real effort was made to get the babies out safely.

At first, every Pan Am flight out of Vietnam would have four, six, eight babies on it. The stewardesses—and stewards, since some were male—would literally smuggle the children on board with the airline's approval and bring them out. As the days went by, it went from six or eight babies, to eighty or a hundred babies on every flight.

At that point, I got a call from the daughter of Joe Daly, the owner of World Airways, a charter airline that flew out of Oakland Airport. It was a commercial air carrier that contracted with the military to transport cargo and GIs to and from Vietnam. Daly called to ask the Red Cross for help because they had a whole planeload of babies coming into Oakland from Saigon the next day.

COURTESY OF THE BAY AREA CHAPTER
OF THE AMERICAN RED CROSS

Several of us went to Oakland Airport to meet the plane after it landed, and the crew started off-loading babies. They were handing babies out the door of the plane and people in the crowd started passing babies over their heads. Some people were grabbing babies and leaving. I was stunned. It was absolutely chaotic.

Then we found out that there were going to be another 250 babies on the next plane coming in. That's when we put out the word that we needed Red Cross volunteers immediately to assist with the orphan airlift.

The General of the Sixth Army at the Presidio, the naval base in San Francisco, said that he would help. He opened up a big reserve hangar for us called Harmon Hall. Here's how the operation was set up: When the planes landed, pediatric residents from the University of California Medical Center (UCSF) went on board the airplanes and performed triage. Sick babies were put in an ambulance and taken to UCSF hospital. Meanwhile the Mayor of San Francisco had given us the green-light to use city buses to bring the babies from planes. We put someone in charge of the buses and put twenty volunteers, along with a Red Cross first-aid instructor, on each bus going to the airport. The first-aid instructor had twenty plastic hospital bracelets with numbers on them. When the bus got to the airport, the Red Cross "registrar" went aboard the plane with the twenty volunteers and they put the bracelets on the babies. Then volunteers carried the babies onto the bus and held them in their laps on the trip back to the Presidio. When each bus pulled away, another bus with twenty volunteers—they were called "laps"—pulled up, and they started on the next twenty babies.

At the Presidio, the laps handed the babies over to volunteer nurses—seventy per shift. Nursing schools and hospitals from all over the area sent students and nurses to take the babies from the laps, wash them, examine them and feed them—and they really needed it! I got on one airplane, a 747, and the flight was empty except for cardboard boxes in every seat. There were three hundred babies—most of the children were infants—in cardboard boxes on that airplane and they all had diarrhea. The stench was overwhelming.

Not surprisingly, the nurses said they needed more bathtubs. I asked a Red Cross volunteer, Juan Hull, to go to the local Red Cross chapter and pick up all the bathtubs used for the mother and baby classes taught there. He came back with three! I sent him to Walgreens to buy all the bathtubs they had. He could only get six more bathtubs. I said, "Do something! We need bathtubs."

Down by the San Francisco airport, there's a big boulevard, Lombard Street that's got a whole bunch of restaurants on it. The volunteer came back with forty bus-boy trays—they are actually like small tubs—and that's what the nurses used to give the babies baths.

We in San Francisco were just a way station for those babies. They ended up at adoption agencies throughout the U.S. Some went directly to specific families that had already been assigned to them, back in Vietnam. Most of the adoption agencies were affiliated with the Catholic Church, since these were kids coming out of Catholic orphanages in Vietnam.

Hundreds of airline stewards and stewardesses volunteered on their days off to help transport the babies to adoption agencies. When the airline staff got off work, they would come to the motels along the Presidio and sleep the night. The next day they would pick up two, three or four babies from the Presidio to take them wherever they were going—on the plane of their next assignment. They loved those babies—some would spend all night holding them, or lying right next to them.

The third or fourth day the babies came into San Francisco, we got word that President Ford and his wife, Betty, were going to fly out on Air Force One to give their blessings to this humanitarian effort. I had been active in the California Young Republicans and Ford came to California often to do fundraising. So I knew that before he was vice president, he had been the Red Cross disaster chairman at a Red Cross chapter in Michigan.

We went to meet them at San Francisco Airport where Air Force One was going to connect up with a Pan Am flight coming in from Saigon. While we were waiting, Dr. Arlene Mann, the Red Cross medical advisor, said that Betty Ford was being treated for cancer, and if she was on chemotherapy she should not be near these babies since we had no idea what kind of vector of infection we might be opening up. Dr. Mann called the White House and explained the situation to the White House surgeon, who said he would radio Air Force One and tell Mrs. Ford not to come in direct contact with the Vietnamese babies.

When President Ford came off Air Force One, I greeted him and I asked if I could please put a Red Cross name badge on him and Mrs. Ford. He said, "You know I am entitled to wear that." I said, "Yes, Mr. President, both as the Red Cross honorary president and as a former disaster chairman."

Betty Ford went from bus to bus visiting with and saying thank you to the Red Cross volunteers before they got on the airplane. She got off the bus before they pulled up to the plane to get the babies. Meanwhile, President Ford, wearing a Red Cross badge, carried out three babies—one for each network, ABC, CBS and NBC—and each TV station ran an exclusive of him handing the babies to Red Cross volunteers.

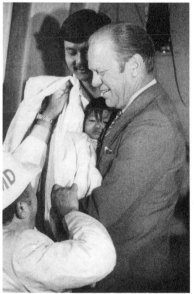

COURTESY OF THE AMERICAN RED CROSS
President Gerald Ford holding a Vietnamese baby, 1975

I remember one planeload that had older children—from toddlers to teenagers—with polio on board. They were headed for a Catholic hospital in Oregon that worked with polio kids. We kept them overnight at the Presidio. The next day they got on a plane and flew up to Oregon. I am old enough to remember when polio in kids was fairly common, but most of us hadn't seen steel leg braces and crutches on kids with polio in years. It was a real tearjerker.

One of the laps stayed all night at Harmon Hall to comfort a boy who was extremely upset. As she got on a bus to take him out to the airport to go up to Oregon, she shouted, "Pete, call my husband and tell him I'm not coming home—I'm not leaving this kid until I see that he's safely taken care of." She got on the airplane, flew up to Oregon with him and helped him get settled in at the adoption agency.

After about the second or third week into the operation, the military wanted to speed up the process of getting the babies out of Vietnam. The air force assigned a C-5A, a huge military lift airplane to pick up five hundred babies from the air force base in Saigon, and bring them to San Francisco. They had five hundred babies and the medical records from seven or eight different orphanages loaded on a C-5A in Vietnam. On takeoff it crashed and burned.

One hundred seventy-two people died.

The next day we had some babies who had survived the C-5A crash come in on a Pan Am flight. One baby had a piece of metal in his head so the pediatric doctors put him in an ambulance and rushed him to UCSF Medical Center. They performed surgery, but he died. That was really bleak for all of us.

At that point, we realized that these kids had no paperwork recording their admittance to the United States, since most of their medical records were burned on the flight that crashed. We worked with the Presidio Military Police (MPs) to create an official American Red Cross entry document. The MPs took a Polaroid picture of each baby and rolled a footprint. We put the footprint and the Polaroid on Red Cross letterhead with a note saying the American Red Cross had received this baby, on this day, under the Red Cross orphan airlift, and the number assigned to them on their wristband since we didn't know their names. This piece of paper was the only record these kids—who are now adults—have to document their admission to the U.S., and it was sent with the escorts to the adoption agencies for the adoptive parents.

After the orphan airlift ended, the Red Cross recruited six hundred of the nurses who volunteered during the airlift to become Red Cross nurses for future assignments, and it welcomed many other new volunteers into its ranks. Late that summer Pete Ashen spent seven weeks at Camp Pendleton Marine Base in southern California working on a Red Cross operation to help relocate more than 100,000 Vietnamese refugees to the U.S.

In addition to teaching many disaster classes, Ashen established the

Disaster Institute at California State University in Sacramento in the late 1970s to provide disaster training to Red Cross staff and volunteers, and the Disaster Preparedness Information Council, which continues to put on disaster preparedness conferences in San Francisco.

Ashen retired from Red Cross staff in 1994 in San Francisco, where he lives with his wife, Catherine. He has two children and two grandchildren.

He continues to volunteer on local and national disaster assignments. After September 11th, he volunteered as a check signer at Pier 94 in New York City. Ashen signed 4,500 checks for a total of $2.5 million for victims and family members of the terrorist attacks.

Jennifer Young
Gun Barrel City, Texas

When Jennifer Young was in grade school in the 1950s and junior high in the 1960s, her mother, Dotty Gene Young, was a full-time homemaker. Twice a month, Young's mother would don a Red Cross uniform, a blue dress with white shoes, and register donors at a Red Cross bloodmobile. Young's grandmother was also a Red Cross volunteer who rolled bandages during World War I.

As a child, Young also learned how to swim from a Red Cross instructor in Webster Groves, a suburb of Saint Louis. She went on to swim competitively and as a teenager, became a Red Cross certified swim instructor. At Purdue University in West Lafayette, Indiana, she heard about the SRAO program in Vietnam, and immediately looked into joining.

I went off to college in 1964 and I really didn't think that much about the Red Cross. Then my junior year, as I was moving back into the Delta Gamma sorority house, the chat was, "Did you hear what Kitty did? She joined the Red Cross and is now in Vietnam." When you're in a sorority, you have to remember the major, hometown, boyfriends and boyfriends' fraternities of the upper classmen, so I knew that Kitty had *not* majored in nursing.

The minute I found out that someone with a college degree could

COURTESY OF JENNIFER YOUNG

join the Red Cross and go to Vietnam, I knew this was what I wanted to do when I got out of college. I was female so I knew I would not be drafted. The war was horrible and I wanted to do something to help.

I had the good fortune of having the Midwest office of the Red Cross right in Saint Louis, my hometown, so I applied and I went for an interview. I learned that you had to be a college graduate, and I was still a junior. Since I was spending my senior year in Madrid on the year-abroad program, I applied in advance so I would have a job lined up when I came home.

I was the oldest child of three, and the only female, and by then, my parents were accustomed to letting me do what I wanted to do. For example, when I graduated from high school, I went off to be a camp counselor and lifeguard a hundred and fifty miles away, and then I went to college three hundred miles away, and when I was in college, I told them I wanted to do my senior year in Europe, and after I finished that, I wanted to join the Red Cross and work in Vietnam. So my parents did not panic. The Red Cross, by virtue of its reputation, gave them a certain sense that this was legitimate.

The SRAO program had specific criteria you had to meet—you couldn't just be some romantic star-struck teenager just out of high school. But it still was romantic to me. To tell the truth, I had seen some World War II movies and I thought the soldiers were neat and needed comforting. I watched South Pacific and I saw the nurses and I wanted to be a part of it— just like a lot of the men saw a lot of John Wayne movies and wanted to be soldiers. I did not have the intestinal fortitude to study nursing, but I wanted to do this, I wanted to be around it, I wanted to see that part of the world and I wanted to see what was going on.

I went for the romance and adventure of it. A lot of male senior college students I knew were about to lose their student deferment· and many of them didn't want to go to Vietnam. Slots on the National Guard and in the reserves were few and far between, and a lot of college men were trying to get in there.

I got back from Europe in the summer of '68, I took a two-week training class in Washington and then I left for Vietnam. When I was a rookie, I was assigned to a unit in Dong Ba Thin. It is on the mainland side of Cam Ranh Bay, a huge installation on the east coast, which was the headquarters for the Eighteenth Engineer Brigade for Special Forces and for a unit of Special Forces.

We staffed an on-base recreation center there and it was a unit that also had mobile assignments, which meant we took our homemade recreation games out to the field. We visited Tuy Hoa Air Base and its surrounding army units of the 173rd Airborne, and Phan Thiet, where the 101st Airborne was stationed. We always traveled in pairs, and we had enough staff to have two groups of two go on forward runs while two stayed behind. A forward run meant going to an outlying encampment of some kind, like a landing zone or firebase—where artillery, big tanks and cannons are set up to support what's going on around them. In many cases, the men's surroundings did not include any kind of recreation, such as a USO or Special Services club, or a Red Cross recreation center.

The land was beautiful, very green and lush, but most of the places we landed had been cleared off to build a firebase or landing zone. An infantry unit will come back to a firebase after being out on patrol to relax, sleep or get a change of socks—that was their base of civilization.

COURTESY OF JENNIFER YOUNG

Jennifer Young with members of the Fourth Infantry Division of the U.S. Army in Vietnam

The firebase was very arid without any foliage or grass—just dust and maybe a little asphalt. There was a big square area full of sandbags and bunkers and a lot of tents. Most times the site was very primitive, and the men were living underground in bunkers. Other places were a bit more built up, with barracks or a mess tent. There were lots of sandbags around the buildings, anchoring down the corrugated tin roofs, and a lot of dirt, mud and OD—everything was olive drab—the vehicles, the weapons and the men's fatigues. Our assignment was to visit the troops who were out there in the boonies, at firebases, and lighten things up for them. We mainly traveled in helicopters to get to the firebases and landing zones. Of course, I would have given anything to ride in a Cobra, but if we were photographed in a gunship or holding a weapon, the photos could have been used as proof that the United States and the American Red Cross were not adhering to the Geneva Convention of Red Cross personnel being non-combatants. I would have been sent home immediately.

Being around the military was amazing. Some of the things I was exposed to—the chopper rides, spending the night in places I really shouldn't have been—it was a real adventure. You figured, if my number comes up, my number comes up, but I'm going to have a good time meanwhile and do my job, and help the guys out, and see everything and do everything and be everywhere that I possibly can.

At the same time, I think we were a security risk. Some men probably had to stick their necks out further than they might have otherwise just because they had a woman on board. Besides, we wore these light blue Dacron uniforms—those bright blue dots stood out against everything else that was dark, dirty, grimy and muddy—we were like beacons. On one hand, that's good because the men knew that there were females on the base. But at the same time, there were rumors that the Viet Cong thought we were excellent sniper targets—two little blue dots running around with no flak jackets, no steel pots [helmets]. Although I don't know of any cases where a sniper tried to take out a "Donut Dollie." The only time we came under fire was when the whole area was under fire.

On one run from Dong Ba Thin, I had to spend the night at Bao Loc because we got fogged in. Rain and fog would sometimes prevent aircraft from flying. Sometimes a pilot might think he could get us back home, but he would have to turn back because he couldn't see. Sometimes a typhoon alert would ground all aircraft.

Female overnights were unheard of at a place like Bao Loc, so someone really scrounged to find a place for us to spend the night. I slept on a cot with mosquito netting in a tent with wooden floors. Two pilots who shared the tent vacated it for the two Red Cross girls. It got chilly so they gave us their aviator jackets for warmth. Then they gave us two toothbrushes, two tubes of toothpaste, two little pans of water, two OD towels—given the time and place, it was the equivalent of a five-star hotel!

It was the night before Thanksgiving and all of the generators were consolidated to feed into the mess tent so the men could prepare the meal for the next day. Everybody congregated at the mess tent because that's where the generators were. They were pulling biscuits out of the gas oven and I remember thinking that when they opened the oven door, you could really smell the gas from the stove. Then everyone starting running outside, and my eyes started watering. One man announced that we had just been CSd and told us to go outside and face the wind and just let your eyes water. CS, I learned, stands for concentrated stuff—somebody had popped some tear gas just for amusement.

I was at Dong Ba Thin two and a half months, then I was moved to Tuy Hoa, further north along the coast, because the air force requested that Red Cross girls be stationed there full time. The day I moved up there, I spent the entire day trying to hitch a ride on an airplane with all of our stuff—a refrigerator, Kool-Aid cooler, cartons of arts and crafts supplies, paperback books, puzzles and games. It all couldn't fit in one aircraft, and I was stuck waiting for the next plane. Finally, an air force pilot who was finished with his missions got clearance to fly me up to Tuy Hoa.

This was the same day the officers' club on the beach at Tuy Hoa was having its grand opening party. They had flown a bunch of nurses up from Cam Ranh and they were wearing these long, floral, pretty dresses. All of the women were in civilian party attire.

Tuy Hoa had previously been a destination we flew into for two-night stays from Dong Ba Thin. No women had lived there—the four Red Cross women coming to Tuy Hoa to live would be the first and only women on the entire base. Because I arrived late, I was whisked to the party as soon as the airplane landed. I was in uniform with a bandana on my head, sunburned from waiting on the tarmac all day and I was dirty. So, I was the only obvious Red Cross girl—my co-workers had arrived earlier and had changed into civilian clothes. Besides, I was easy to spot because I'm six feet tall and blonde!

I could not believe my eyes. I could not believe how plush the officers' club was—it was on the beach, it had a sunken bar, a stage, candlelights, and a dance band and dance floor. I had been used to the army, where all you saw were olive drab fatigues. The air force fighter squadrons each had their own unique party flight suits, usually a bright color with a coordinating ascot. There were bright red suits with white ascots, black party flight suits with burgundy ascots and powder blue party suits with red ascots—and they all had beautiful embroidery and patches.

I was only in Tuy Hoa a month before they transferred me to Cam Ranh Air Base, which was on the mainland side of the bay. The base was so big that there were two recreation centers. Cam Ranh had a huge army installation and a huge air force installation, side by side. The air force side looked like suburbia—all the buildings were close together, all lined up, and it went on for acres. The streets were paved and there were sidewalks and streetlights and it felt like you were in the States—it was all-American. The army side was more primitive.

I was in Cam Ranh more than three months. We stayed in a long hut, an entire compound of females, so there was a lot more partying with dances, invitations for barbeques, steak fries and luaus, and movies at the club. There was a beautiful beach nearby with white sand and clear blue water, and a truck would go around as if it were a scheduled bus and take you to the beach. You could be at the beach for a while and catch the 2:15 truck back to the base to work a shift.

At Cam Ranh I was Red Cross program director, which was the number two spot in a unit. The program director schedules shifts, schedules runs, and makes sure that everyone is progressing according to a timeline, whether they're making their props or developing a program for the road.

But I still went on runs. On another trip back from Bao Loc, I was in a Chinook with one of my fellow Red Cross girls named Julie, and the aircraft was diverted and called into action to extract some troops from a "hot area" where there was enemy activity. Some troops were being fired upon; they had retreated and were waiting to be taken out. "I can't," the pilot responded. "I've got two Delta Deltas on board." We were referred to as Delta Deltas, DD, Donut Dollies, in the military alphabet. Since ours was the only aircraft in the area, the pilot was instructed to get us into steel pots and flak jackets and go in.

It was going to be a while before we got there, and it was the end of the day and I was really hungry. The tail gunner, who could walk to the end of the aircraft, asked me if I wanted some food. He took some C-rations, put them up above on the manifold at the back where the engine was real hot, warmed them up and served them out of the can. It tasted so good because I was so hungry. And I thought that was the ultimate in a flight attendant—a gunner on a Chinook in his Nomex suit [a special fire retardant material they wear in helicopters] serving me C-rations before we went into a hot area.

I envisioned getting there and welcoming these troops in, and I was so excited to be involved. As it turned out, we extracted ARVNs [Army of the Republic of Vietnam]—South Vietnamese troops. We didn't even speak their language and they had no idea what our purpose was. I was glad it wasn't our troops who were in danger, but the romance wasn't quite there.

For twenty-seven years, I had been telling people I had never been under fire, except when we had to go to the bunker for incoming. Then in 1995, I found out that I had been. On a trip to Vietnam with a group of women, Julie Pence (now Julie Van Matre), who traveled with me on the tour, told me that when we were in the Chinook, she was on the two-way with the pilot and heard some pings. When she asked the pilot, he said it was small arms fire hitting our aircraft!

I was promoted to unit director, and sent to Camp Enari, headquarters of the Fourth Infantry Division. Camp Enari was a big installation in the central highlands, outside of Pleiku, at the foot of a defunct volcano cone covered over with foliage. We were a hundred percent mobile, and so we visited the forces that were stationed all over the highlands.

It was my favorite assignment. Our quarters were in Quonset huts, we had a non-flush latrine with a shower next to it. The sidewalks that connected our quarters to the latrines were covered by a corrugated tin roof because the monsoons were so bad. I liked the rougher, more primitive assignment because it reminded me that there was something else going on outside the party atmosphere when we were entertaining the troops.

When you're assigned to a group or unit like the Fourth Infantry Division, you get to wear the patch of the infantry division on your uniform. That patch became very important, and when you associate with a division, there's a special place in your heart for those guys. Some girls may have had assignments with several divisions and they had to switch patches, but this was my one and only patch.

In all of the assignments, I had this wonderful feeling of being one of them and we were all in this together. Sometimes I felt like I was just basking in this wonderful treatment, in the chivalry, and the sweetness—I was treated like a queen.

But it was a real paradox because some of the men just assumed that we were there to be call girls for the officers—which was a huge shock for me. You had the sense that they liked you, but deep down, they wondered what you were really doing at night. I only got propositioned once, and it was by an enlisted man who wasn't even subtle about it—he just assumed that receiving a proposition was something I was prepared to do, because that was the business I was in.

Of course, the Red Cross put curfews on us, but there were USO females, Special Services females and others who did not have curfew. A lot of time their conduct would spill over—every female that was not in the military in Vietnam was assumed to be a Red Cross girl. Somehow, when the story was told the next day, it always became a Red Cross girl that was partying all night. And so a Donut Dollie could really toe the line and still wind up with a reputation.

True, some of the women did some cozying up, but the ones I saw really cared for the guy. Some of the girls were in love. One Red Cross girl got married in Saigon at the end of her tour to an air force pilot she'd met.

As unit director, I had to handle rumors about my staff. Though there were rumors that some of the girls got paid for sex, there's not anybody I suspected of doing that. You would try to get to the bottom of a rumor but you never could. The only thing you could do was transfer that particular young lady, and let her start all over again.

Realistically, when you have a program that sends close to seven hundred women to Vietnam over seven years, can every person say no one did anything? You can only answer for your own experience. I developed some favorites, and guys that I really, really liked—there were a few of those. But when you have four or five assignments in twelve months, you're not in one place long enough to really have a love affair. I realized that we were in an artificial environment where you can't even really date. You couldn't be sure your feelings would hold up back home. You'd wonder if it was true blue or just an infatuation. So at each assignment, I had a favorite person who said, "Come on over, and can I buy you dinner at the Officers' Mess?" or "Can we spend an afternoon on the beach together?" I had those, but nothing beyond that. I went over a virgin and I returned a virgin.

When Jennifer Young returned from Vietnam in November 1969, her father suggested that she "do something practical to make yourself marketable." Since she already knew how to type, Young took classes in shorthand in Chicago before moving to Dallas.

Young found a job in the personnel department of Mobil Oil Company, and she spent the next twenty-five years in human resources for large companies in Dallas, Boise, Idaho and Santa Barbara, California. Young says her experience in Vietnam helped her understand and navigate the male-dominated corporate world. She applied her knowledge of military rank to the workplace. "If you only knew what I've seen and been through and done," she recalls thinking to herself. "Man, you've got nothing on me." After 9/11, Young decided that she wanted to work toward retirement, and in September 2003 she retired to an east Texas lake to live with the man who's been her significant other since 1987.

Throughout her career, Young made time for the Red Cross. In the early 1970s, when she was living in Dallas, she served as a personnel consultant to the local chapter, and volunteered to escort Vietnam veterans, mostly amputees, who were hospitalized at the Veterans Administration Hospital, to local events like the circus, concerts, musicals, or out for pizza. In Boise, she was a disaster services volunteer and served on the board of directors of the chapter there. Now that she's retired, Young hopes to update her disaster training and respond to national disasters.

Katheryn Courville
Longview, Texas

In 1998 Katheryn Courville was working in sales and marketing for a hotel chain, a job she had held for seven years, when she had an epiphany. She was thirty-five years old, and she wanted to change her life and do something she deemed more worthwhile and fulfilling. So she quit her job and went to work for the Red Cross—even though it meant taking a $10,000 pay cut. As a single woman, she knew this would mean a certain lifestyle change but she was looking for more than a salary from her job. "I decided that if I was going to be paid to do something, I wanted it to be worthwhile and for a good cause."

Already a volunteer for the Volunteer Services Committee of the American Red Cross of Central Texas in Austin, she applied for a job in special events and fundraising. She considers taking the job the single best decision she's ever made. "After working for fifteen years, I finally felt good about what I was doing every day I walked into work."

During the four years Courville worked at the Austin chapter, she signed up for almost every class offered—disaster, health and safety, babysitting and CPR classes. Her goal was to go out on a national disaster assignment—and someday, to fulfill her dream of working on an international relief operation.

Courville was finally called out on a large-scale disaster after September 11th. She worked with the International Family Assistance Program in Washington, D.C., to assist the families of hundreds of foreign nationals who had died or were missing in the World Trade Center. Courville's experience in the travel industry came in handy since the job entailed arranging transportation and hotels for victims' family members. Shortly after that, she left her Red Cross job and went back to school to get a nursing degree.

In January 2002, Courville was asked to attend training in Honduras to become a member of the International Response Team (IRT)—an elite group of highly trained Red Cross professionals. A little over a year after she graduated from nursing school, a deadly tsunami hit southeastern Asia on December 26th, 2004. When she saw the extent of the damage on the news, Courville contacted Beth Casey, at the International Disaster Relief Unit (IDRU), the international arm of the American Red Cross. "I want to go," she wrote in an e-mail.

Two days later, Courville informed her supervisors at work that she would be gone for a month. "In my mind, I thought, this is so much bigger than my emergency room nursing job. It's too big to pass up and I have to go," she says. It was noon and her flight to Washington, D.C., for debriefing was at six o'clock the same night. When Courville handed in the application for a leave of absence at work, she was told that it would be submitted to the higher-ups in a few days. "I said, 'I'll be back in a month and we can talk about it then.'" That night, Courville left for her assignment in Sri Lanka as a delegate of the International Federation of Red Cross and Red Crescent Societies.

Four of us landed in Sri Lanka on January 1st—Matthew Parry, our team leader, and Stacy Ragan, both paid staff members from International Services in Washington; Ron Matthews, a volunteer from Iowa; and me from Texas. We were called an Emergency Response Unit (ERU). Our job was to make sure that the goods donated by the various Red Cross societies were delivered to the people who needed them. We also had to account for every dollar so that every country that contributed was assured that whatever they donated went where it was supposed to go.

COURTESY OF CHARLES BLAKE

Handing out sheets near Hikkaduwa on the southwestern coast of Sri Lanka

When a disaster happens in another country, the local Red Cross makes an appeal to the International Federation of Red Cross and Red Crescent* Societies, the international network of national organizations. They list exactly what they need—for example, one hundred thousand blankets, twenty thousand tents and a dollar amount. That appeal goes to all of the 181 Red Cross and Red Crescent societies—the worldwide network of national and international aid organizations that use these symbols. The individual organizations choose to respond to the appeal either by sending money or people to the country to help out. The American Red Cross did both—sending money as well as people.

In a case such as the Sri Lanka tsunami, once the appeal goes out, the various societies send donated items to the affected country. Federation delegates claim them at the airport, store them until they can be transported to where they are needed, and then distribute them with the help of the local Red Cross Society.

ERUs from different countries take on different responsibilities. In Sri Lanka, the British Red Cross handled logistics. The Spanish handled telecommunications. The German Red Cross flew in a hospital unit—a one hundredperson hospital with doctors, nurses, medicine and equipment.

We handled distribution. We were sent to a town called Galle (pronounced "Gawl") in the southern province. It's a highly populated resort area for Europeans, and since it was winter—the high season—there were a lot of tourists, Swedes and Germans there for vacation.

The Sri Lankan coast is absolute paradise with white sand beaches and palm trees. But we never saw anyone go in the water. The local residents would not eat any fish that came from the ocean because of the belief that there were many bodies in the water that the fish were eating. By the time I got there, they had recovered most of the bodies, except for those trapped inside a passenger train that had run parallel to the coastal road. When the wave came in, the train was stopped in the middle of the village. People got on the train because they wanted to get away from the water. The force of the water overtook the train and toppled it on its side. More than a thousand people were drowned in the train alone.

In Galle, I was the systems delegate, responsible for finances and logistics for our team. The first item on my "to do" list was to set up the office at the warehouse. It was right on the coast and had been hit by the tsunami, so there was no electricity and the telephone lines were down. I spent some time trying to get the satellite phone to work, trying to get e-mail, getting a fax and copy machine set up, and organizing all of the office supplies. The Spanish delegation had to make several trips to our site because I was having so much trouble setting up this operation.

Once that was done, I dealt with paper flow, and I helped the warehouse manager, Jim Stephenson, an American who was working with the British ERU, organize the shipments of supplies coming in from Colombo, the capital, and going out daily to be handed out. We had to enter everything into an Excel spreadsheet, so we could account for everything. We also had to report exactly what we were doing back to the federation and the donors.

The Red Cross may be a bureaucracy, but at least our distribution methods keeps in mind the dignity of our beneficiaries. No one has to beg, no one has to jump over other people, or get trampled in the process. It might take us longer, but the people know they're going to get everything their neighbor has. Our system is fair and equitable, and doesn't create a sense of panic.

While we were there, we saw terrible, terrible means of distribution. The worst one is what some call "truck and chuck," and we saw this happening all the time. A truck slowly drives down a main road and somebody inside throws stuff out. Anybody who happens to be on the road can get whatever is being dropped off that day. People sat along the road all day waiting for a truck to go by, and then there would be a stampede. "Truck and chuck" is fast and quick—at least it gets necessities to some—but it creates an atmosphere of panic.

While I was there, I learned first-hand the power of the Red Cross and Red Crescent symbols. Every day we wore vests with the Red Cross on it, and we were treated like royalty. Our driver was pulled over once because he was talking on a cell phone, which is illegal in Sri Lanka. The policeman was going to give him a ticket, but when he saw that we were Red Cross, he let us go. I imagine that the children who saw us wearing that symbol are going to grow up thinking that the Red Cross is a great organization. That's because it stands for those seven principles that all of us within the Red Cross know so well— humanity, impartiality, neutrality, independence, universality, voluntary service and unity.

I'm fortunate that I was able to go and do what I did. There are ninety-nine jobs in relief aid, and I had the best one. I actually got to hand out the goods to the people. The Sri Lankans are such a beautiful people, and they are so friendly. Everyone always smiled, and they were so gracious and grateful. People would look up and say, "thank you" in their best English. You can't ask for a better feeling in the entire world than that.

When I did casework locally in Texas and handed out vouchers to people at fires and floods, it was the same feeling. That's why I became a nurse—I want to help people hands on, to work directly with them, because I personally get so much out of it. It energizes me. It makes me feel good. It's like a high—I have to do it.

When Katheryn Courville returned to her nursing job after a month, she learned that not only was her unpaid leave of absence approved, but the hospital posted an announcement that anyone who wanted to donate their own paid time off could donate it to make up for her lost salary. "When I came back, I had a full month's salary waiting for me," she says.

After Courville and the original American ERU team left Sri Lanka, two more teams were sent from the American Red Cross. In Sri Lanka alone, 36,000 people died; the total death toll in Asia was 225,000 in eleven countries. Americans responded by pledging $535 million to the Red Cross in the aftermath, all of which was earmarked for emergency and long-term relief programs. As a result, more

COURTESY OF KATHERYN COURVILLE
"There are ninety-nine jobs in relief aid, and I had the best one," says Courville.

than 400,000 people received American Red Cross relief supplies in Sri Lanka, Indonesia and the Maldives. In addition to providing mental health support and vaccinating thousands of children, the Red Cross, via a partnership with the World Food Programme, a UN agency, provided food to some 1.7 million people in the region, and continues to do so as we go to press. The Red Cross has also initiated long-term relief programs, such as a water sanitation program in Sri Lanka that will assist more than one million residents.

Part II

—

THE EYE OF THE STORM

Chapter 3

THE CALL OF THE RED CROSS

I was a "thousand points of light" long before volunteerism lighted up the sky and had an official name. I had my lights short-circuited, burned at both ends and occasionally punched out. I hang in there because generally volunteerism is a dazzling galaxy of gems that streak across the sky and illuminate the world when it falters and cannot find its way."

—From Being A Volunteer – A Noble Profession, *by the late Erma Bombeck, humorist and Red Cross volunteer with the Southern Arizona chapter in Tucson, Arizona*

Ever since President Theodore Roosevelt signed a congressional charter in 1905, authorizing the American Red Cross to provide emergency relief when disaster strikes, Red Cross workers have been on the scene of every major disaster in the country—and millions of smaller disasters. The Red Cross was there in 1906, when the infamous San Francisco earthquake and ensuing fires killed more than seven hundred people. The Red Cross was there in 1935 when a ferocious hurricane devastated the Florida Keys. The Red Cross was there in 1969 when Hurricane Camille, a category five hurricane, caused 256 deaths along the Mississippi Delta, and again in 1972 when Hurricane

Agnes caused severe flooding from Virginia to New York.

The Red Cross was there in 1989 when Hurricane Hugo ravaged Puerto Rico, the U.S. Virgin Islands and Charleston, South Carolina, then three weeks later, when a temblor measuring 7.1 on the Richter scale tore apart San Francisco. The Red Cross was there in 1992 when Hurricane An-

COURTESY OF THE AMERICAN RED CROSS
Hurricane Camille's 190-mph winds and 22-foot storm surge leveled Pass Christian Mississippi in 1969

drew—until Hurricane Katrina, the largest and most costly natural disaster on American soil—wreaked havoc on Dade County, Florida.

The Red Cross was there in 1995, five minutes after a bomb tore apart the Alfred P. Murrah federal building in Oklahoma City. The Red Cross was there after the terrorist attacks of September 11, 2001, and in the fall of 2004, when four back-to-back hurricanes crisscrossed Florida and the Gulf Coast in a six-week period.

As I write in the fall of 2005, more than 210,000 staff—mostly volunteers—from all fifty states have been on hand in Louisiana, Mississippi and Alabama in the aftermath of Hurricane Katrina, which tore through the Gulf Coast on August 29, 2005. The hurricane, which killed at least one thousand people and cut a swath of destruction more than ninety thousand square miles, amounted to the largest mobilization of Red Cross personnel to a disaster in history.

What compels these people to head toward a disaster area just as most residents are trying to escape? Why do they do it for years, sometimes even decades? What hooks them into a life of such service and dedication?

People who do disaster work are altruistic. But there is more to it than that. The internal reward of knowing that you made a difference cannot be overemphasized. Listen to volunteer Peter Teahen, a funeral director from Cedar Rapids, Iowa, who has counseled many grieving families at mass casualty incidents. "Being on the scene of a disaster and counseling people challenges me personally and makes me feel like I'm contributing, helping people through a very difficult time," he explains. "Even though my work can be extremely stressful, what I do has incredible value in a time of crisis."

Virginia Stern, a social worker and Red Cross mental health volunteer in New York City, adds that disaster work is exciting. "People who volunteer for disasters like the rush they get from working a disaster," she says. "On a disaster, they're important and they're doing something that matters. We all want to do things that matter in life."

Some have likened the Red Cross to a secular religion in the way its people follow, and even embody, the organization's mission and the seven fundamental principles of the Red Cross movement. The 20th International Conference of the Red Cross in Geneva adopted these principles—humanity, impartiality, neutrality, independence, universality, voluntary service and unity—in 1965. "We have a great mission and it's like a magnet to people who have a passion for compassion," says Harold Brooks, CEO of the Bay Area chapter in San Francisco.

Red Cross Board of Governor member and disaster volunteer Ross Ogden agrees. He points out

COURTESY OF THE AMERICAN RED CROSS

In 1989, Hurricane Hugo caused severe damage to the U.S. Virgin Islands, then continued towards the East Coast, where it made landfall in Charleston, South Carolina

that the common thread among the members of the Red Cross movement worldwide is that they believe in the seven fundamental principles. "Those are fundamental beliefs that people who join the organization not only subscribe to, but they become great motivators," he says. "The barriers to entry are very low, but the motivating factor is very high."

Most people remember exactly when their passion for Red Cross work was born. Genny Sheridan, a volunteer nurse from Baton Rouge, Louisiana, heeded the call during World War II, when as a junior Red Cross volunteer at age fifteen, she rolled bandages for the troops. At age seventy-nine, she has been to more than forty disasters.

Dr. Susan Hassmiller's parents were on a trip in Mexico City in 1974 when a news flash on TV broadcast that a significant earthquake had occurred there. In a panic, she dialed the operator, who connected her to the American Red Cross. Her local chapter couldn't tell her that her parents were okay, but within twenty-four hours, someone got back to her. "She said that there were no fatalities, and the hotel where my parents were staying was perfectly intact. But the telephone lines were down and as soon as the phones were running, she was sure that my parents would call, and they did," Hassmiller recalls. "I thought, *My God, what on earth kind of organization is this that told me that my parents were okay?!*" Hassmiller joined up soon after, and has been involved with the Red Cross as a volunteer, or paid staff member, since then. She is currently a member of the Board of Governors.

Harold Brooks became enamored with the Red Cross on his first disaster assignment in South Central Los Angeles in 1975 while he was working for the United Way, which was, and still is, involved in a partnership with the Red Cross to raise money. "I fell in love with the organization because I saw all these selfless volunteers helping others in their hour of need," recalls Brooks. "It really started my romance with the organization and it's continued ever since—in fact my commitment is renewed every time I go out on a disaster assignment."

Once they become a part of the organization, disaster workers gain entrée to a world unto itself, with its own culture and lingo. They drive and dispense food from an

COURTESY OF THE AMERICAN RED CROSS
Hurricane Andrew caused $25 billion in damages to Dade County, Florida in 1992

"ERV" (an emergency response vehicle). Most spend some time on the local "DAT" (disaster action team). Then they are called out on a national disaster through the "DSHR" (disaster services human resources) system—a huge database of paid staff and volunteers trained to respond to disasters nationwide.

It is through these national disasters that many volunteers have built a community of friends—and some even consider the Red Cross their second family, particularly retirees who make up a significant portion of disaster volunteers. "Are you Red Cross?" is a common question those in the organization's ranks ask of folks they meet.

Many collect Red Cross memorabilia. They wear Red Cross jackets, shirts, hats and vests, as well as service pins that indicate their years of service, the disasters they have been to, or how many gallons of blood they have donated. And once a year, Red Crossers congregate at the national convention, an annual pep rally where they renew ties with the friends they have made through the years, and celebrate the good works of their beloved organization.

As staff grow older they eventually retire from disaster work, and some leave sooner for various reasons. When dealing with large-scale disasters, the organization is structured to recruit new volunteers, called LDVs—local disaster volunteers—to funnel new blood, so to speak, into the ranks. LDVs are responsible not only for recruiting other local volunteers, but also for providing essential manpower and knowledge of local logistics to allow the relief work to function smoothly. It is common for disaster victims—once they get back on their feet—to offer their services as a way of repaying the organization.

After the Oklahoma City bombing in 1995, there were some nine thousand spontaneous local disaster

COURTESY OF THE AMERICAN RED CROSS
A building destroyed by the Northridge, California earthquake in 1994

volunteers, according to Debby Hampton, CEO of the Oklahoma City chapter. And after September 11th—six years after the Oklahoma City bombing—the Oklahoma City chapter sent fourteen people whose families had been directly affected by the bombing to New York City with the goal of turning their own tragedy into a way to help others. "They had been through so much and we struggled with deciding if it was a good idea to ask them to go," says Hampton. "But we found that it made them much stronger." In the aftermath of Hurricane Katrina, the Red Cross launched an unprecedented program to welcome thousands of new volunteers into its ranks. These people were trained and deployed to affected areas in a matter of days. Many of these people, who had no prior affiliation with the Red Cross, repeated the same mantra, "I felt I had to do something," and the Red Cross became the natural conduit for their charitable acts.

Jean Zinnen, a registered nurse from Morrison, Illinois was among them. After Katrina came ashore, she heard about a five-hour Red Cross disaster training class from a colleague. "We called the Red Cross on Friday, trained on Monday and left on Tuesday," recalls Zinnen. Her husband was on a fishing trip in Canada. She signed up, and left her husband a note on the kitchen table saying that she was going to Louisiana to help out. She spent the next three weeks living and working in a shelter in a basketball arena at Southern University in Baton Rouge. She dispensed over-the-counter medicines, put in IVs, and evaluated residents who needed hospitalization. When her twelve-hour shift ended, she slept on a cot in the shelter alongside three nurses who also traveled with her from Illinois. One night, a security officer cautioned the women to sleep behind a concession stand to avoid sniper fire. Earlier in the evening a gang member who had assaulted a young man was thrown out. He yelled that he was going to get his buddies and come back and shoot the place up. Zinnen—who taped her grown children's pictures on the wall next to her cot—didn't lose a wink, confident that the eighteen national guardsmen who patrolled the shelter would keep the staff and shelter residents secure.

Fortunately for the Red Cross, and the people affected by the killer storm, there were tens of thousands of Americans like Zinnen with a burning desire to be useful to the relief effort. New Yorker Stern sums up their value this way: "What the volunteers do is useful, but the fact that they simply go do it—be at the scene of a disaster, in the middle of the night, under difficult conditions—means a great deal to the people they are helping. This is what makes people feel safe and cared for. It is this spirit that makes the Red Cross . . . the Red Cross."

Rolla "Bud" Crick
Portland, Oregon

By the time Bud Crick was thirty years old, the Red Cross had lent him a helping hand not once, but twice, something he kept in the back of his mind during the next four decades while he pursued his career in journalism. Crick helped launch Stars and Stripes *in Tokyo as a GI in World War II, and joined the* Portland Journal *after he returned from the war, spending the next thirty years there. After the paper merged with* The Oregonian, *he stayed another twelve years before retiring in 1989. His job took him to more than one hundred countries, and his paper twice nominated him for the Pulitzer Prize. In 1994 Crick became a volunteer with the Oregon Trails chapter of the Red Cross in Portland.*

After a lifetime as a newspaper reporter, he found himself on the other side of the fence, so to speak—handling public affairs for the Red Cross on disaster relief operations. Crick has volunteered at floods and wildfires in his home state of Oregon; floods and tornadoes in Tennessee, Louisiana, Kansas, Alabama, Kentucky and Minnesota; and Hurricanes Georges (1998), Bret (1999) and Floyd (1999), to name a few. After September 11th, Crick spent fifty-seven days in New York City on three separate assignments, and was there every month from September through March.

COURTESY OF THE AMERICAN RED CROSS OREGON TRAIL CHAPTER

The day I went into the Army in 1944, my wife said good-bye, went to the hospital and had our son the same day. They told me that when I was through basic training at Fort Lewis in Denver, I could go back and spend some time with my family. Meanwhile, I got transferred to Randolph Field in San Antonio, and that's when the Red Cross came to my aid. I made twenty-one dollars a month, but with the Red Cross's help, my family joined me in Texas, and then came with me when I was transferred to Monroe, Louisiana. It was fairly well known that the Red Cross was able to help people this way. I think the Red Cross purchased the train tickets for my family. It must have been an outright gift of some kind because I don't remember ever paying anybody back.

The next time the Red Cross assisted me was after I was discharged from the service and returned to Portland in 1948. When I came home from the service, I moved into a housing project called Vanport City—midway between Vancouver and Portland—because it was low-cost housing.

It was on Memorial Day weekend, 1948. Let me explain the geography so you can understand what happened. Vanport City was located near the Columbia Slough, a low, swampy area located a few hundred yards from the river. The Columbia River drains into the Colorado River basin three states away. The river fills up with water that rushes down in the spring from the mountains on the Oregon side of the river—Washington's on the other side. That winter there was a lot of snow, and the snow pack was deep, going all the way up into Canada, and now it's spring and it's raining cats and dogs, and the snow pack is melting, and you've got a flood.

Anyway, all this water poured down the Columbia River into the Vanport City housing project in Portland. This was before all the dams were there. On one side of Vanport City is a railroad fill that acted as a dyke—that's what broke and allowed the waters to pour in on one side. On the other side of the city was a highway, again on top of fill, which isn't that stable, and the water filled up a depression in the ground, and broke its way through the highway. The first night I saw some of the buildings flowing through that break. It was the middle of the night, and you could see these big two-story apartment buildings floating down the river. It was a disastrous flood. Eighteen people were lost.

My family was visiting relatives down in Eugene, in the middle of the state, and so they were out of town at the time. I was sent out to cover the flood for *The Journal*. I went out and stayed there all day and night, and most of the next day and night, mainly working, covering what was happening for the paper. I kept going back to the office to write stories.

Fortunately, the apartment building we were in stayed put. Our apartment was on the first floor. Before it was too late, I went inside to grab what I could get. I had another newsman stand outside the door and tell me when I had to get out. I grabbed a box of papers, and that's really all I got out with because the floodwaters were arriving—all I saw was the froth of water—and so I got out.

It was more than a month before the water went down enough that I could get into our building again. And when I did, everything was ruined. Our apartment was flooded completely, and water had gotten pretty close to the second floor. An overstuffed chair had a toadstool growing out of it. Mud was everywhere. Some things weren't there any more—doors and windows were broken and gone. I carried out some clothing, but there wasn't much I could salvage. My uniforms from the war were ruined so I got rid of them, and I've been sorry ever since. I was one of the first American soldiers into Hiroshima and I had lots of mementos from the war, and all of that was lost.

Of course, the Red Cross did what they still do today—met with victims and gave them emergency assistance. Red Cross gave me some vouchers so we could acquire some bedding, clothes and groceries. It's short-term assistance, to try to get people on the road to recovery.

When my family returned, one of my coworkers at *The Journal* took us in and let us stay at their place until we could get a house. With the help of the newspaper, I was able to purchase a house rather soon, within six weeks or so after the flood. Because of that, I didn't need a great deal of assistance from the Red Cross.

From that time until 1994, I didn't have any other contact with the Red Cross, except covering them as a newsman. They were part of my rather large beat—I covered military, aviation, courthouses and crime, and I did feature writing too, along with some travel pieces. When I covered Red Cross, it was what they were doing in the local community, their fund drives or the blood program.

My wife is a retired nurse, and a few years after I left the paper, she said, "Why don't we go down and join the Red Cross?" So we did, and we started taking all the courses—Introduction to Disaster Services, Family Services, Mass Care, Damage Assessment and Disaster Public Affairs.

As a member of the local disaster action team (DAT), I was on call at all times—and a lot of disasters happen at two in the morning. I've done dozens of local disasters over the years, including some rather large apartment fires. Almost from the beginning, I went out to those disasters in a dual role. I did family service, which entails meeting with clients, listening to what they need and providing whatever services we're able to—food, shelter and clothing. And because of my background, I also met with news media—I wore both hats at all times. The Red Cross was happy to have a newsman come aboard. I joined the DSHR—the staffing system for national disasters—in 1995, but I also remained a member of the DAT on the local level.

Working with the media for the Red Cross is on the other side of the fence from what I did for most of my life—instead of being a probing reporter, I'm taking pictures and writing stories for the Red Cross. Actually, disaster public affairs is a three-way job: We work with the media to get the Red Cross story out; we support the other functions of the Red Cross, such as producing flyers explaining where shelters and service centers are located, and any other information victims need; and we also act as an advocate for victims—we talk to them and find out what needs aren't being met, and help them get in touch with the people who can help them.

That was particularly the case after September 11th. For example, after we had been in operation for a couple of months, we heard of an Arab community that lived near Ground Zero. They were immigrants. They were afraid to come forth to seek any help. When you become aware of a problem like this, you help get them in touch with the people who can help. After 9/11, I not only wrote press releases about what was going on and what the Red Cross was doing, I helped set up interviews with victims for the media. Getting the word out that the Red Cross is helping people is definitely part of my job.

All disasters are full of gripping stories—dramatic and traumatic—of humans in trouble. I may have a victim who is willing to talk to media who has a great story to tell. I'll explain to the reporter something about the story and the person, and I try to get the reporter to understand that he has to work carefully with this person who's just suffered a loss, and if he does so, he will probably get a good story. The reporters appreciate that we're helping them find the very thing that they're looking for, and the victims know we represent the agency helping them, and so they trust us when we bring media to them. Mainly it's a case of persuading people that media is not as bad as they think—if they give them a chance, the media can help them. So it works out well for both sides.

I was in Puerto Rico for Hurricane Georges in 1998, and I was assigned to Arecibo up on the coast. I went with the family services team down into the middle of the island where a town called Utuado had been covered with water. I did two things there: I helped family services do casework, and at the same time I interviewed victims, looking for human-interest stories to feed to the press. A number of the merchants in that small town became upset that the Red Cross was sending everyone to Kmart. They came up for a meeting at Arecibo. It got to be pretty hot for a while—they were charging that the Red Cross was not doing what it should being doing.

On the spur of the moment I said, "Look, why don't we see if we can solve this some way? Why don't you as merchants get together and put on a festival? You can say the citizens of Utuado and the Red Cross are pulling together attempting to help people. Also, put signs in your windows that you're going to accept Red Cross vouchers. I'll get you some publicity in the local press and I'll take some pictures of you now."

Their whole attitude changed. All of a sudden they all wanted their pictures taken, and they were very cooperative. What had been an angry meeting—it looked like it was going to be bedlam—solved itself. There are a lot of opportunities like that with the Red Cross.

In a way, the Red Cross is just one big happy family. The Red Cross is not just the public affairs person—it's the family services tech, the damage assessment person, the mental health professional—it's all of these different functions, doing what we can to make the situation better.

When a disaster occurs, you're all geared up, you're ready to go. Some of us—like me, I guess—become disaster junkies. That isn't all bad, because the more of these things you go on, the more helpful you can be because of what you've learned from doing it before. After all, the cause of each disaster is different, but the suffering is the same, and so are the needs of the people. You know what you can do to get them on the road to recovery the best way possible, and that always leaves you with a good feeling. You know that you've really helped somebody. I've been working with the Red Cross for a long time, and I'm proud of what we do. When I respond as a representative of the Red Cross wearing a Red Cross insignia, I am showing whomever I come into contact with that the Red Cross is there not to exploit, but to help. That makes me feel good inside because I realize that that's exactly what we're doing—we're helping people.

And that feeds my desire to pay back the good that the Red Cross did for me early on in my life. I think that's what it is all about.

Eighty-seven year old Bud Crick responded to twenty-six national disasters from 1989 to 2003. When he was diagnosed with macular degeneration in February, 2003, Crick retired from the disaster action team because he could no longer drive at night.

Ken Thompson
Oklahoma City, Oklahoma

*A*t 9:02 A.M. *on Wednesday, April 19, 1995, Ken Thompson was sitting in his office in Oklahoma City, where he worked as vice president of a local credit union. At the same time, two and a half miles away, Timothy McVeigh detonated a 4,800-pound bomb in a truck parked in front of the Alfred P. Murrah federal building.*

All of the windows in Thompson's office shook violently. Thompson thought a car had driven into the building.

When he looked out, he saw smoke rising from downtown. He turned on the TV, and watched as newscasters announced that an explosion had blown apart one of the two federal buildings across the street from each other in downtown Oklahoma City. One was the federal courthouse. The other was the Murrah building, where Thompson's mother, Virginia Thompson, had worked in the credit union the last three months. The bomb killed 168 people, including Virginia Thompson. She was fifty-six years old.

After his mother's death, Thompson became involved with the nascent National Memorial Institute for the Prevention of Terrorism (MIPT), established in 1999 to prevent and combat terrorism, and assist first responders on the scene of terrorist attacks. In the weeks after 9/11, Thompson spearheaded the effort to bring fourteen Oklahoma City residents who had lost loved ones in the 1995 bombing to New York to help families affected by the terrorist attacks cope with their losses. The support was, in part, to reciprocate for New York's altruism after the Oklahoma City bombing, when members of New York Task Force One, an elite search and rescue team, was on the scene the next day to help with the recovery effort. The work of the task force created a unique bond between two otherwise disparate cities. On April 19, 2005, forty-four family members who lost relatives on September 11th attended the memorial services in Oklahoma City on the ten-year anniversary of the bombing. The other reason for sending Oklahoma City residents to New York was simple altruism—to help out where needed. Thompson made two promises to himself back in 1995—"to make my mom proud of me every day, and to give back to the people who helped us," he says. "I would hate to think I would have to live through losing the most important woman in my life at the time and not be able to give back from that pain."

When I turned the television on, I saw the live view of the Channel 9 helicopter come around the front of the Murrah building, and I knew my mom was dead. I saw the front of the building, which was blown away, the smoldering ash, the powderized wallboard and concrete, and right across the street there were cars burning.

I knew exactly where her office was—she was on the third floor and she was on the north side of the building. And the north side was gone. I just had a feeling in my heart that she was gone from my life. My mom never missed work, she was a person that was always on time—so I knew that she got there at 8 A.M. In the pit of your stomach, you know that your mother should have been in that area and that that area was completely gone. Of course, you hold out hope against hope that maybe she is still alive—that maybe she was sick that day, maybe she went to the restroom, or maybe she stepped outside to help somebody—there's no telling.

I called my brother Phillip, who also worked in the downtown area, and my sister Shelly, who was at home, about thirty miles away. Phillip went down to the Murrah building to try to locate my mom. He circled the building and could not find her. Since I knew where she parked, I told him when he called from a cell phone to start looking for her car. He found it and placed a business card on the car and wrote a note to her. Then he came

COURTESY OF KEN THOMPSON

back to my office, where my sister and sister-in-law had all gathered. My sister was twenty-six, I was thirty, and Phillip was thirty-two.

Later that morning, we went to my home, which was not far from the Murrah building. My brother and sister stayed there trying to get in touch with other family members across the U.S. I went down to Saint Anthony's hospital, about eight or nine blocks away from the Murrah building, and I began to search for my mom. I spent from about 11:30 A.M. to 5 P.M. at Saint Anthony's.

While I was there, I met one of my mother's coworkers, a teller named Joe, had gotten out of the building safely. I said, "Joe, did you see my mom this morning?" He answered, "Yeah." I asked, "Do you know where she is?" He said that he had seen her in the loan department. I asked where the loan department was located. He said, "Ken, it's on the other side of the hall and it's gone."

The medical examiner's office announced they were going to set up a family assistance center at First Church on 36th and Walker, and that family members could begin arriving after 5 P.M. The media told us—family members—to gather as much information about our loved one as we could. So we took a picture of our mother off the wall of my house, and on the back wrote all of the information about her—height, hair color, eye color. Then we went back over to the family assistance center and turned that in.

We stayed there most of the evening and in the following days we spent a lot of time in a room at the church. We had teams of doctors and nurses in a first-aid area, so if we needed something, antacid, Tylenol, or bandages, that was provided. And of course, we were fed. After the first day, the Red Cross took over the center. It was my first experience dealing with the Red Cross on a personal level. Huge poster cards from communities all across the United States hung from the rafters and allowed us to view what the nation was thinking—their thoughts and wishes—which was very comforting. People donated a lot of books. I picked up a copy of *When Bad Things Happen to Good People*. It had been signed by the author. This book has provided me with a great deal of comfort.

Celebrities came—Kirstie Alley sat with my family for probably an hour—just the sweetest lady in the world. She didn't want the publicity—the only reason she was there was to let us know that people were thinking about us, and that somehow made a tremendous difference.

What was particularly beneficial to us, number one, was that security was very tight—Red Cross personnel were at the front desk making sure everyone was appropriately vetted to come into the family assistance center. Number two, the mental health teams and clergy—what Red Cross calls spiritual care—were allowed to come in. We had a lot of Red Cross staff just sit with us at tables. Now there are pluses and minuses to that. Sometimes mental health personnel can be a little bit overwhelming. Some of them have a tendency at times to stick a tissue in your face and ask you to talk about your feelings, and that can be the last thing family members may want. It can be very, very uncomfortable. We certainly had some other problems in Oklahoma City. When we came into the family assistance center that first evening, we were confronted with people from a funeral directors association—their badges read: "Funeral Director." We weren't ready for that. It was only about nine hours after the explosion. The following day their

COURTESY OF KEN THOMPSON

Ken Thompson and his brother Phillip just before the
Alfred P. Murrah federal building was imploded, May 1995

badges read, "Medical Examiner Support Personnel"—which wasn't as harsh as seeing the words "Funeral Director." Another problem: It took a day or so to move the media away from the venue. Photos taken of family members—including my own—were too raw.

The family assistance center in Oklahoma City was open for seventeen days. On the evening of May 4th at 11:45 p.m., seventeen days after the explosion, they called off the search for survivors. The building was deemed unstable. At the time, they believed there were two individuals still in the building that they could not get to because of the way debris was piled against a pillar—I remember the number exactly—pillar twenty-two. If they had continued to remove rubble out of that pile, the building might have collapsed.

The following morning, May 5th, my family was called to the family assistance center. A number of bodies had been identified that morning, and all of the families were called up at that time. About an hour after we arrived, we learned that our mother's body was one of the two bodies left in the building. Due to the instability of the building, there was a less than fifty percent chance that we would ever be able to get her back. Ray Blakeney, the public information officer for the medical examiner's office, had gotten close to my brother and me, and he could not come and tell us because he was too upset. Instead, Tom Demuth, a funeral director who had volunteered as a liaison with the medical examiner's office, broke the news. When he told us, he began to cry. Every time we see him, we still hug him.

We were allowed to go down to the site the following morning. I have a photo of my brother and me in the rubble laying a wreath as close to our mom as we could. Demolition teams imploded the building several days later. When they went back into the area, the workers actually located three individuals. Christi Roses, a young lady who had worked in the building two or three weeks, was identified the day after Memorial Day. She was trained on the telephone system by my mom. They were not aware that a gentleman named Alvin Justice was in the building—he was identified the following day. My mother was the very last person identified on June 1st, forty-three days after the event.

I felt a tremendous amount of leadership coming from our city, from the medical examiner's office and from the Red Cross. I've never needed assistance in terms of mental health or any monetary need, but just knowing that the Red Cross was there for me has been a great help.

A group of us in Oklahoma City started the National Memorial Institute for the Prevention of Terrorism in 1999. I was asked to become an advisory board member. After we began to heal here in Oklahoma, we formed an outreach committee, made up of family members, survivors and responders, all who would be able to help others in case there was another attack on America anywhere.

In 2000 we went to Israel for ten days and we met with victims of the ongoing conflict in the Middle East, both Palestinian and Israeli. Ten people participated—all except me were survivors of the Oklahoma City bombing. One evening in Tel Aviv, we met with about twenty Israelis who had suffered terribly in various ways. We went around the room and each of us talked about our loss. Each person was able to communicate, if they were comfortable, how their loss happened (a gentleman served as a translator). We got about three-quarters around the room, and there was a man whose son and wife were killed, and he was partially blinded by a Molotov cocktail. He said, "For the first time in twenty-six years, I am able to talk about this because you came here." We spoke for two and a half hours. It was very emotional, with lots of hugs and tears.

It was the beginning of our understanding that losing someone to terrorism—the pain, agony and despair—is the same, regardless of ethnicity, religion or societal issues. We found that the bond is unbelievable in terms of giving people resilience and hope—and we knew that in case another terrorist event happened, we could give back.

Then on 9/11, I watched on live TV when the second plane came in. I had to relive Oklahoma City for the first hour or so, and I just could not believe what was happening. I started thinking to myself, "What are family members doing in New York and Washington, and the people affected by Flight 93 that went down in Pennsylvania? Were they going to hospitals and searching for their loved ones like I did?"

I called General Dennis Reimer, the director of the National Memorial Institute for the Prevention of Terrorism, and a retired chief of staff of the U.S. Army. Since this is based in Oklahoma City, I was able to meet with him at 1:00 that day. We discussed how family members and survivors from Oklahoma City could assist those affected by the attacks that morning. He said, "I know that the Pentagon can take care of itself, so I want you to focus on New York City."

Next, we put something on our Web site offering our assistance. It said that if you'd like to speak with a family member or survivor of the Oklahoma City bombing, feel free to reach out to us. Within twenty-four hours, a lady by the name of Cathy Miller sent an e-mail. It read: "Are any of you coming to help us? God knows you know how we feel. My father, Robert Kennedy, is lost in Tower One. We need your help."

That's when we began trying to get to New York City. One of the Institute's board members at the time, Cheryl Vaught, was also a board member of the Oklahoma City Red Cross. I spoke with her and Debby Hampton, the Oklahoma City chapter CEO, and said that we have something unique to offer. We can give direct family assistance from people who have been through the same kind of tragedy. Debby made a call to Jane Morgan, director of individual assistance, at Red Cross national headquarters, and she authorized approval for two people to go to New York to work with the Red Cross. Six days later, on September 17, Diane Leonard, who had lost her husband in the Oklahoma City bombing, and I went to New York City to begin working in the family assistance center on Pier 94. Two days after I arrived in New York, Cathy Miller, the lady that originally reached out to Oklahoma City after 9/11, came into the center. She had lost her dad, Robert Kennedy. We spent two hours laughing and crying. It began a huge friendship. Since then, she has come to Oklahoma City every April 19th—the anniversary of the bombing—and I have been to New York every 9/11. We have even taken vacations together with our families, my wife, Shannon and our children, Faith and Hope. It's been a blessing to all of us. We have a relationship that will probably never end. We are all part of a club that no one wants to join. Cathy likes to say that we are bonded by tragedy and united in sprit.

Over the next weeks and months, we sent three family members from Oklahoma at a time for a maximum of seven days. We sent a total fourteen people who lost loved ones in Oklahoma City to New York. They were all volunteers, hand-picked by their ability to have already moved through the grieving process and not have an agenda. We didn't want anyone going up there trying to be famous or trying to do anything outside the margins of what was set up with the Red Cross. We were doing something that had never been done before. I had no Red Cross training, but by practically living in a family assistance center for seventeen days in Oklahoma City, when my mother was missing, I received all the training I would ever need. I think we understood the tragedy from a completely different perspective than someone who has not been through one himself.

What was key was to make sure that we didn't seem like Oklahoma City was coming to the rescue. We weren't there to do anything other than to let people know that they may be able to work through their grief and love life again someday, because we have been able to do that, one way or another.

We were there for three reasons: First, we were there to give family members resilience and hope. That is what we felt we owed the people of New York. Second, we were able to show people who work within the Red Cross and other non-government organizations that what they do makes a difference—I'm living proof of this. Diane Leonard and I went to the Brooklyn chapter almost daily to let the staff know their work makes a tremendous difference, even though they may not work directly with family members. It's not often they get to talk to people who have lived through a disaster of this sort. Finally, we could help the Red Cross understand the most appropriate ways of helping family members caught up in a tragedy like this.

At first, we worked behind the scenes—for example, we urged Mayor Guiliani's (then mayor of New York City) office to encourage the coroner's office to issue death certificates. From our experience, you can't begin grieving until you have a death certificate. In Oklahoma City, seeing "homicide" on the death certificate moved me along in the grieving process.

We also wanted to make sure family members were able to go to the site. It was important for my family and me to go to the site—a television doesn't do justice to the devastation. It's difficult to get a handle on it unless you see it firsthand.

I remember in 1995 thinking that maybe my mom got knocked on the head and she somehow got out. But the day they called the search off, I was able to go to the site and place flowers down—and for the first time, I got it. I looked at the building and said, "She didn't get out." That's exactly what we wanted to do in New York. This was two to three weeks after 9/11, and there were some people who still had hope that their missing family member was alive. But when you view six stories of rubble still on fire—like the families in New York did—you're basically allowing them to accept that their loved one didn't get out.

The family members of those missing were taken by boat from midtown at Pier 94 to the site. Before we got on board, Lt. Grace Telesco, of the New York City Police Department, introduced everyone who would be on board—the mental health professionals, the EMTs, as well as us, the family members from Oklahoma City. We had people on every single boat.

When the 9/11 family members got on, everybody knew who we were—simply people who had been through a similar circumstance. We weren't overbearing. We never walked up to anybody and asked, "How are you feeling today?" We never said that we "know how you feel." And we never told people how to grieve. We weren't there trying to fix anyone—we knew they were not broken, they were grieving. They approached us and bombarded us with questions: "Is it okay to cry? Will I ever get over it? When is the first time you laughed?" What we really wanted them to know was that they would make it through this someday, but each of them had to find their own path.

The boat traveled down river to a dock near the site, and then we all walked the two blocks to a viewing platform. The police security guard kept the media away, and made sure that no pictures were taken of the family members. The boat carried fifty family members at a time, three times a day for about seven weeks.

Ken Thompson traveled to New York twenty-six times in the first three years after 9/11 to work with American Red Cross national headquarters, the Greater New York chapter of the Red Cross, the New York City mayor's office and family groups. Like most of the volunteers from Oklahoma City who came to New York, Thompson signed up for formal Red Cross training in several areas when he returned to Oklahoma City, and he ultimately became a Critical Response Team instructor. In December 2001, Thompson quit his job at the credit union to become director of external affairs for the Memorial Institute for the Prevention of Terrorism.

He has also been involved in the planning, establishment and construction of the Oklahoma City National Memorial and the Memorial Museum. Thompson was selected by New York City Mayor Michael Bloomberg, the A&E Television Network to receive the 2002 Biography Community Hero Award due to his outstanding service to the City of New York in the months following 9/11. In 2005 the President's Council on Service and Civic Participation selected Thompson for the President's Volunteer Service Gold Award for his commitment to strengthening the nation and making a difference through volunteer service. "I have a huge desire to give back and it's incredibly healing to do so," he says. "If it weren't for the compassion of this nation and the people who came to help us in April 1995, I would not be where I am today and I wouldn't be nearly as resilient."

Teresa Palazzo
Arlington, Texas

Teresa Palazzo spent the first twenty-eight years of her life living in an apartment in the Bronx. In September 1994, Palazzo and her family moved to Texas because her husband, Carlo, who works for General Motors, was transferred. Soon after, the family built a ranch-style home in what's known as the Dallas-Fort Worth metroplex, an urban area that lies in the heart of Tornado Alley—a swath of more than a dozen states prone to deadly tornadoes.

Palazzo knew nothing about tornado preparedness and she worried that a tornado would hit while she was home alone with her two children and her husband was at work. He worked at the General Motors Assembly plant.

A few tornado watches and warnings had been issued during the first five years they were in Texas, but Palazzo's community was always spared, so she put it out of her mind. One day, Palazzo met a Red Cross worker who taught her what to do to protect her family in the event of a tornado. That chance encounter ulti-

mately saved their lives. She remembers the day precisely.

COURTESY OF TERESA PALAZZO
Teresa Palazzo and her daughter on the one-year anniversary of the tornado, 2001

On Saturday, March 18, 2000, there was a safety fair in our neighborhood at Williams Elementary School, where my eight-year-old son attended school. My husband and

I decided to stop by. They had different booths set up, a fire truck and all sorts of activities for the kids. We came across the Red Cross booth and I thought, "Here's the Red Cross, let's get some information about tornadoes." I started talking to a woman named Anita Foster about tornadoes, and we discussed how to figure out a safe place in your home, what supplies to have on hand, and what to do once a tornado hits. I was there for quite a while, and by the time I left, I knew my family's safety plan, and where to go in our home in case it ever happened to us.

Ten days later, my worst fear came true. An F3 tornado ripped my house apart. Tornadoes are categorized F1 through F5, and an F3 tornado is severe, with wind speeds from 113 to 206 miles per hour. At winds like that, trees are uprooted and roofs are torn off of even well-constructed homes.

Just like I had feared, my husband was working the night shift, three to midnight. My two kids, Michael, who was eight at the time, and Nicole, who was three, were playing outside. I was chatting with neighbors. The kids commented on the "weird-looking sky"—it was green. It started to rain, so I called the kids inside the house. They sat down to eat dinner, and we turned on the TV to watch the weather. An alert on the news broke in that said "Fort Worth tornado warning." Then I began getting phone calls from friends and neighbors, and that is when I began to get the mattress and other items ready near the linen closet—our safe place to go hide.

Then all of a sudden, the lights went out. My son, who had done duck-and-cover drills in school, said, "Mom, we should take cover." I knew what was happening, but I guess I didn't want to believe it, and I just kept telling him, "It's a really bad storm." He said, "No, no, I think we should run to the closet." I said, "Okay," and as we were running, the tornado hit.

I got the kids to the linen closet just in time, and we had everything we needed—flashlights, blankets, extra batteries and a cell phone. I had stocked the linen closet after I attended the talk at the safety fair. The linen closet is right off the living room. My bedroom closet is behind the linen closet, so it's framed in really well, and there are no outside walls. It's the only place in my house where we could go because we have no basement.

Nicole and Michael were able to sit on the floor underneath the bottom shelf, because you're supposed to stay low to the ground. Both of them fit in there. I grabbed a crib mattress, put it over me, and I was lying in the doorway, just inside the closet with the door closed. When the tornado came through the house, it was really hard to hold that crib mattress on top of myself.

It was 6:56 P.M. when it hit. It only lasted about four or five minutes, but it felt like forever. We heard all sorts of sounds—glass breaking, windows shattering, the sound of the house being ripped apart. It sounded like a train was coming through our house. We heard things hitting the house and water seeping through the light fixtures and ceilings. It was dark. Michael was very nervous—we were all nervous and scared. I told them it would be okay, but it was the most frightening night of my life.

Afterwards, I was in shock. I cried. I was scared to come out, but I left the closet when I started to hear neighbors calling me from outside to see if we were okay. A neighbor guided us out our front door because there was so much debris and wood, and it was dark and you really couldn't see anything.

We went to his house, and we waited there for my husband to come home because I didn't want to stay in my house alone. I really didn't pay much attention to how bad the damage was, I just got out of there. But I did notice our house didn't have a roof. The neighbor's house didn't have a roof either and we could see the sky and stars.

My husband weathered the storm at a shelter in the plant, and he came home as soon as he learned that our area was hit. He had called and I told him we were okay, but he wasn't prepared for what he saw when he drove home. It looked like a bomb

COURTESY OF TERESA PALAZZO

Palazzo's neighborhood after the tornado

hit the neighborhood. Some houses had more damage than others. Ours was badly damaged, but it wasn't a total wreck. The roof was gone, there was lots of water damage, broken glass, wood and debris all over the place. Michael's room was totally destroyed—everything in it was gone. Glass and wood were embedded in the walls and bedding. Things had flown into my house that belonged to neighbors. We found someone else's lamp, Nicole's baby blanket and our pots and pans in front of our house, in back of our house, in other rooms in the house. The fences were gone, the swing set in the backyard had been lifted and moved several feet away and twisted up like a pretzel. All the windows were blown out and a two-by-four came in through the roof that shot right through into my garage.

The next morning, representatives from the restoration company and the insurance company came. They told us to grab clothes and necessities, and go to a hotel. They packed up everything else and put it in storage. Some homes had to be knocked down and rebuilt, from the ground up, but they were able to fix ours.

After three days in the hotel, we stayed with friends until we were able to move back into our own house—four months later.

For weeks the Red Cross came around every day with a food truck, called an ERV—an emergency response vehicle. They fed us every morning, afternoon and night. They also passed out shovels, brooms and other items that we needed. In fact, they were in my son's school, where a Red Cross shelter was located, every day, with items for people to come pick up. My daughter Nicole's bicycle was destroyed by the tornado, and the Red Cross gave her a new pink one. That was the first time she smiled in days.

The Red Cross was always here—they never left us. Six months after the tornado there was a celebration, behind the school, and the Red Cross was there again. That's when I reunited with Anita Foster. She knew immediately who I was. We hugged and cried. We became instant friends and I began volunteering right after that.

I volunteer at safety fairs with Anita, and when people ask questions about tornadoes, Anita says, "Well here's the person to talk to—she experienced a tornado, and she's not even from Texas!" I tell them about my experience, and educate people about where to go, what to do, what's the safest place in their home, and what they should have packed in an emergency supply kit. My children are there with me—they sit and talk to people and other kids, and pass out brochures.

On March 28, 2001, one year after the tornado hit, we held a celebration on our block. Anyone and everyone who had helped us out throughout that time came out—the fire department, the police department, local businesses, schools, churches and the Red Cross. I helped Anita make a slide show presentation, and we had drinks and pizza donated for the event. Mainly it was for the neighborhood to thank everyone who was out there for us. It had taken a year to rebuild our homes, and the neighborhood was back to looking normal again. A local business had t-shirts made up that said, "We survived the tornado." Another neighbor and I made up flyers and passed them around the neighborhood asking for donations to the Red Cross. We collected $1,800.

Although our neighborhood has been spared a tornado since then, one did come down in Mansfield, just ten miles from home. My whole family and some neighbors went to the tornado site to volunteer. We helped clean up yards and handed out food and supplies. Some people just wanted someone to talk to, and ease their minds a little bit. We could actually say, "We understand what you're going through—we just went through it."

Until this happened to me, I never realized how much the Red Cross does. And they never forget you. They are always there—caring and compassionate people—when you need them. I thank Anita and the Red Cross for all they do and for taking the time to talk to me on March 18, 2000, and to teach me what I needed to know about tornado safety. If it wasn't for them, I don't think I would have been as prepared as I was, and my kids and I might not be alive.

Palazzo continues to volunteer in various capacities with the Red Cross. She organized Masters of Disaster, a tornado safety course for students in kindergarten through sixth grade at her son's school, where a large percentage of students were affected by the 2000 tornado. Her latest project is making paper dolls to help teach children at safety fairs about Red Cross lifesaving programs, and tornado and fire safety. In September 2002, Palazzo received a Public Awareness award from the Chisholm Trail chapter of the American Red Cross. She was also featured in a Woman's Day *magazine article entitled "I Will Survive," about women who turned a personal tragedy into a way to help.*

Elda Sanchez
Miami, Florida

Elda Sanchez had hit rock bottom in 1992. She finalized her divorce in March and lost her job in April. In May, she moved in with her sister, who lived in Perrine, a small town located near the Everglades between Miami and Homestead. Sanchez began to look for a job and a place to live. On August 24th of that year, Hurricane Andrew made landfall near Homestead, fifteen miles away. With peak winds of 172 miles per hour, the category five hurricane destroyed a record 25,000 homes, and damaged another 100,000—including Sanchez's sister's home.

The disaster seemed like the latest calamity to strike her already tenuous existence, but the tragedy—and more specifically, the help she received from the Red Cross afterward—helped turn Elda Sanchez's life around.

I was out of town and when I came back to Homestead after the hurricane, I couldn't find my sister's house. I was driving through the neighborhood, and all of the main streets were closed, so I looked for landmarks. When I left two days before, it was a beautiful neighborhood of single-family homes, some ranch-style and some two-story homes. But everything was destroyed—all of the trees were down, the roads were torn up. It took me four hours to find the house.

Finally, I saw my nephew, who lived with us, standing in front. When I asked him where the house was, he said, "Right there." He pointed to a house with a

COURTESY OF THE MIAMI CHAPTER
OF THE AMERICAN RED CROSS

missing roof, no garage door, no landscaping, no garden. Everything was destroyed. The inside of the house looked terrible—all of the windows were broken, and everything was wet—the carpet, the mattresses, our clothes, the furniture. It seemed like the end of the world to me.

I had moved to Miami from Cuba in 1971 with my husband and two young children. But I had just gotten divorced, and my family was very upset with me. I lost my job as a clerk in a grocery store. I had so many problems back then. I was thinking of killing myself.

I moved to Homestead to get my feet back on the ground, and then came Hurricane Andrew—and I lost everything I had. My furniture was in my sister's garage, and the water just poured in when the door blew off. Everything was ruined. We had to throw away the mattresses, carpets and our clothes. We didn't have electricity for more than four months so it was impossible to wash our clothes, and they got moldy and had to be thrown out. I lost all of my pictures and other personal things—all the memories I have from my children when they were little—we had to throw all of that away, too.

The Red Cross opened several shelters, but we refused to go because we didn't want to leave what was left of our belongings. We were afraid they would be stolen. We decided to stay in the home because the National Guard came right away, and they stayed in the neighborhood and took care of us. There wasn't any looting in our neighborhood. Red Cross workers also came with the ERV and fed us twice a day. We went down to the corner and waited for the truck like kids wait for ice cream!

A neighbor told us to go to the Red Cross and apply for assistance. I had never heard anything about the Red Cross before. When I went to apply, the family service caseworker saw that I was very depressed, and she immediately called someone who worked in mental health. Two Red Cross mental health workers personally drove me in a Red Cross car to a local health clinic. That impressed me. I said to myself, *"How come these people are so nice?"*

After that I went by myself to the clinic in Homestead, because the doctor had to see me often. I was treated with both medications and counseling. Of course, the Red Cross also provided vouchers for clothing and groceries, and they gave me a referral so I could get my medicine paid for.

Two weeks after the hurricane, I went to volunteer my time to the Red Cross at one of the service centers in Homestead. I had several volunteer assignments over the next months. I started out registering new clients and after that I worked as a translator—many of the disaster victims were Spanish-speaking. Then I worked on records and reports on an ERV. I filed all the disaster registration forms, which provide the Red Cross with a case record for each client; filled out the vouchers to make sure the vendors got paid; and I tracked the number of cases we had. Then I sent everything to national headquarters.

I stayed on as a volunteer until Red Cross national headquarters closed the post in Homestead several months after the hurricane struck. I heard that the South Miami-Dade branch of the Miami chapter in Homestead was looking for an administrative assistant for the branch manager, and I interviewed for the job and was hired. I worked with them until 1996, when the Red Cross closed the branch due to financial problems. Then I was sent to the Miami chapter, where I did health and safety customer service—we scheduled CPR, first-aid and swimming classes.

The Red Cross reopened the Homestead/South Dade County branch in 1999, and when the branch manager resigned a year later, I was asked to cover the office until they got someone to fill the position. My coworkers and members of my community here—they know me, and they decided that I had to stay here. They convinced me to apply for the job. I did, and I got hired, and that's how I became Red Cross branch manager in Homestead. The experience I had during hurricane Andrew—as a victim who actually received assistance from the Red Cross—has helped me to do my job as an employee. When we have a big disaster, I remember how grateful I felt. And when we say things like "We are here for you," and "You are not alone," I really know how clients feel and what they are going through. When you are a victim, you think nobody cares about you, but the Red Cross did care about me.

As a branch manager, I am responsible for fundraising. Getting community members to participate, and even donate money, has been easier than it might be otherwise because of everyone's experiences with the Red Cross after Andrew. Most folks are like me and remember. We have a good reputation down here. The Red Cross is known as the one that is present all the time.

Once I got back on my feet, I bought a new house in Miami. People say, "You look different—what happened to you?" I take care of myself, I am a very happy person and I am very happy with my job. I feel so proud. Actually, I feel perfect—I am another person than I was before. It seems odd to say it, but Hurricane Andrew and the Red Cross turned my life around. The Red Cross saved my life.

In 2005, Elda Sanchez was stationed in Miami, where she fielded calls to the hotline made by people affected by Hurricanes Katrina and Rita.

Ross Ogden
Greenwich, Connecticut

In 1960, during Ross Ogden's junior year at Brunswick School in Greenwich, Connecticut, a children's dentist named Richard O'Leary taught a first-aid course to the high school students. Ogden and two friends signed up for the course.

Before long, Ogden was a member of a newly formed first-aid group, a blood donor and a founding member of a high school service club. "The Red Cross, then, as now, has a way when they find a volunteer, of involving them in many things," chuckles Ogden, who has been a volunteer ever since.

Over the years Ogden has worked on dozens of local and national disaster assignments, taught countless first-aid courses, spearheaded community fundraising campaigns and held many leadership positions, including election to the Board of Governors at national headquarters. Ogden refers to his forty-four years with the Red Cross as "some of the greatest experiences of my life. The people I've had a chance to work with, as well as the clients that I've had a chance to serve, and the parts of the country that I've had a chance to see," he says, "have really been extraordinary experiences that I will always remember and wouldn't trade for anything."

COURTESY OF HELEN NEAFSEY
Ogden on assignment after floods in Pennsylvania, 1996

It was the fall of my junior year at Brunswick School in Greenwich, Connecticut. Dick O'Leary had recruited students from several other high schools to take the first-aid course, and it was a way to meet other kids our age in town. There was a lot of hands-on, practical experience in bandaging and resuscitating, and that put you in very close, fun competition and contact with other kids your age—particularly girls. It was more of a social experience than anything else, and since Brunswick is an all-boys school, it was a hit.

O'Leary was a charismatic and gifted leader with kids—he knew how to attract us, how to get us really excited about what we were doing, and how to keep us. He had been a member of the Bethesda-Chevy Chase rescue squad in Maryland, which was one of the premier first aid and rescue squads in the United States; he had a great deal of field experience, actually doing first aid, not just teaching it or talking about it. Whereas I had thought of first aid as putting Band-Aids on cuts, Dick really was talking about first aid as treatment for major trauma, which, when you're a teenage boy, is an interesting topic.

After the first-aid course was over, O'Leary said to us, "Look, you've learned all this material—why don't you do something with it?" He was forming something called a "First Aid Detachment" in Greenwich that would be a backup to the established first-aid providers. Well, that was pretty appealing to a teenager—it sounded like an important task and a way to use some of the skills that we had learned.

One of the first things that O'Leary did was provide us all with uniforms. We wore jeans, but we each got a special gray shirt that had patches on it to show our level of Red Cross training. We were just getting our driver's licenses at that point, and we got a

COURTESY OF ROSS OGDEN
Working at the Connecticut State Emergency Operations Center in Hartford, 1982

special sticker from the Red Cross that went on the back of the car that identified our vehicle as a mobile first-aid unit. All the trappings were there!

The squad actually got to use some of the skills we learned. In the spring of my senior year, there was a bad house fire not too far from my home, and, as a member of the First Aid Detachment, I went and stood by at the fire. The house was pretty much fully consumed. Several firemen were overcome by smoke, and so I began to provide first aid under the direction of the fire department physician and medical examiner in Greenwich, a man named Dr. George Tunick. Dr. Tunick knew Dick O'Leary and what he had done with us. When he saw me in my uniform with my first-aid kit, he summoned me over to help.

He put me in charge of a triage area, taking care of firemen who were overcome by smoke or who had had minor injuries. I was doing heavy-duty first aid while the ambulances were summoned to take some of the firemen to the hospital. For the most part, it was basic trauma care, cleaning and bandaging cuts and flushing eyes for cinders. Because of the smoke, these men were having trouble breathing, so we also administered oxygen under Dr. Tunick's direction, and I was also taking pulses and monitoring conditions.

The reason I remember the event so well was that it occurred the evening of the Brunswick Senior-Faculty Dinner. When I showed up late to the dinner, the head of the school, a man named Alfred E. Everett, was extremely upset with me. He proceeded to chew me out up and down for showing disrespect to the faculty, and coming late to this most important dinner. I tried to explain to him what I had been doing, but he was absolutely not interested. I had better just keep my mouth shut—I was lucky I was going to graduate—that was the implication. The next day, however, the local paper, *Greenwich Time,* had a large article on the fire. The picture in the center of the front page was of me in my Red Cross uniform administering oxygen and first aid to a bunch of firemen sitting on the curb outside the burning house. I had an apology from the headmaster the following morning.

I started college in fall of 1962. I went to Swarthmore, and like

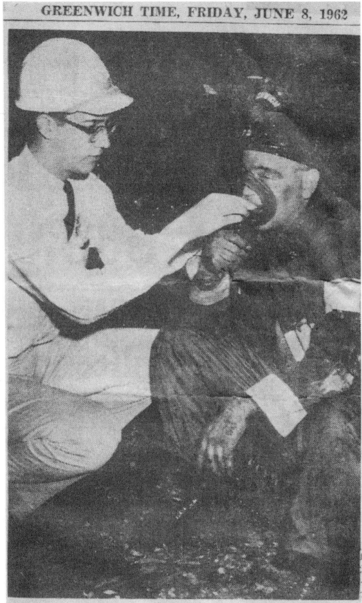

GREENWICH TIME, FRIDAY, JUNE 8, 1962

Receives Aid—Red Cross First Aider Ross Ogden administers oxygen to Fireman Leonard Mingo at the scene of yesterday afternoon's fire on Old Church Rd. Fireman Mingo was one of nine firemen to whom oxygen was administered. The fire, which sent smoke billowing throughout the area, caused an estimated $65,000 damage.—Verderosa Photo

COURTESY OF GREENWICH TIME

Ross Ogden's photo on the front page of the *Greenwich Time*
administering oxygen to a firefighter on the scene of a fire, 1962

most freshmen, I didn't know anybody and I felt a little homesick. But after I got settled on campus, I found the local Red Cross branch and went down and introduced myself. I started out volunteering for a recreation program at the Veterans' Hospital outside of Philadelphia, then I helped organize a blood drive on campus.

As it turned out, in the spring of 1963, the Red Cross national convention was held nearby in Philadelphia and the local chapter asked for youth volunteers. That was a real eye-opener for me. Up until that point, I had thought of the Red Cross as only a very local program, but suddenly, I realized that it was not only a nationwide program, it was a worldwide movement. At the convention, there were people from all over the United States, many of them college-aged like me. It was fascinating to talk to other people who enjoyed doing the same things I'd done, who'd had similar experiences, and to exchange stories and phone numbers.

And, again, it was very social. There were a lot of parties and dances. I remember vividly meeting one extremely attractive girl who, it turned out, was the daughter of a member of the Board of Governors. I didn't know what the Board of Governors was, but as a result of meeting her, I was invited to a lot of the really high level cocktail parties, receptions and tours. I had a ball.

The Red Cross was really now starting to turn into a major part of my life, not only socially, but by giving me a feeling of self worth. When you're a freshman in college, you feel disoriented, that everybody else is smarter than you are, and you're struggling with your classes. But here was something that was familiar at which I could be successful, and I really enjoyed the work, as well as being with friends with whom I was compatible.

I graduated from college in the spring of 1966, and that fall I enrolled in the Graduate School of Business Administration at the University of Virginia. Once again, I was able to take my Red Cross affiliation with me to yet another chapter, this time to the Central Virginia chapter.

I continued to teach first aid for the local chapter. When I finished graduate school, I took a job with General Foods, which was located in White Plains, New York. I had met my wife, Cathy, at Swarthmore, and we got married shortly after I finished graduate school. We moved back to Greenwich, and I reestablished my regular relationship with the Greenwich chapter. At that time, the executive director, Esther Smith, appreciated the value of young people coming into the organization. She encouraged me to take a leadership position, not just to do first aid and the kinds of things I had been doing when I was in school, but to step up and do other things, such as fundraising.

At that time, the Red Cross raised the majority of its money through an annual membership campaign conducted in March—Red Cross month—and volunteers would fan out across town and organize themselves in such a way that every neighborhood was covered by a Red Cross volunteer solicitor. They would go door-to-door, calling on every house and asking for contributions for the Red Cross. It was effective, but it depended on getting volunteers to do it—a huge organizational challenge.

My first job was to chair the apartment division, and I had responsibility for trying to find someone in each of the apartment complexes in central Greenwich. I found somebody in each apartment building to be the captain for that building, and that person had to be willing to get solicitors for each floor of the building.

On Red Cross Sunday, we would go out and knock on all the doors, and then the solicitors would bring the contributions back to the chapter house. It was almost like an election night: people coming in with bags full of checks and money that they'd collected and tallying the results on the tote board, each one bringing us closer to our financial goal.

I also began to teach community first-aid courses and one of the places I taught was the Greenwich Continuing Education program. We offered the course at either no charge or very minimal charge, and I taught it at Greenwich High School in the evenings, from about 1969 to 1976.

The classes ranged from twenty-five to thirty people, with a real cross section of people: mothers who came to take the course because they had young children, Girl Scout leaders, people from a ski patrol, older people who might have a health problem in the family, professional care-givers and non-English speakers, who took it simply because they wanted to learn to speak English better.

Even today, I still run across people that I taught over the years who come up to me and in some cases tell me wonderful stories about a life that they saved, or a situation that they were in where they used their first-aid training. I remember a story of a mother who had been in a pool where there was a near drowning. She gave mouth-to-mouth resuscitation to the child who was pulled out, and it was a successful save. For an instructor, there's nothing better than to hear a story like that.

All the while I was also involved in disaster services. I was volunteering locally at house fires, but in October of 1979, the Greenwich chapter was called to send people up to the Windsor Locks tornado, west of Hartford. It was the first out-of-town, or national, disaster that I was involved in.

I had never seen a tornado before, and I remember driving through the devastated area, which was only a half to three-quarters of a mile wide, but the strip where the storm actually touched down was about seven or eight miles long. It passed through a cemetery, and the winds were so powerful that the turf from the cemetery was literally peeled right off the ground—it was bare earth where the funnel cloud had passed. Granite and marble tombstones had were snapped in half. It was a Catholic cemetery and in the center of the cemetery there had been a huge crucifix. The cross was still standing, but the Christ figure on the crucifix, both the arms and the legs, were snapped off. That's just one of those images that burns into your mind forever.

When you meet the families who've lost their homes—and in this case there were some deaths, as well—you really want to do everything that you can to help them, and you're so glad that you're there. That's the incredible reward of Red Cross work, helping people at a time when they need it the most. It's one of those moments in people's lives when they really are dependent on someone else, and to be there for them and be able to write those vouchers to get them new clothing, to get them a place to stay that's safe, or to be able to reunite a family— that's a tremendous feeling. It's what keeps you going on a disaster.

It's draining emotionally to hear people tell of loss, especially if there have been deaths in the family. But it's so incredibly rewarding to get hugged and sometimes see tears turn into smiles.

In the Red Cross Disaster Services Human Resource System (DSHR) I started off in damage assessment, and I also was trained to be a supervisor in family service. But my real love is administration, and my favorite job is the one that I get to do now, service center manager. The service center is the hub of the relief activity for a particular geographic area, and, as such, you pull together all the Red Cross resources to deliver services. Your job is administration but still close enough to the clients so you get to see and be with them and show them how much you care. I worked as either service center manager, or assistant manager, on three national responses: the southern California earthquake in 1994, the Pennsylvania floods in 1996, and 9/11 disaster relief operation in Connecticut.

One thing that has always impressed me is the diversity of the Red Cross. I've come in contact with all kinds of people I wouldn't otherwise meet—people from the bayous of Louisiana, from South Central LA and the mountains of West Virginia.

Most people, when they talk about Hurricane Andrew in 1992, remember the devastation in south Florida, Miami and Homestead—that was where the vast majority of the damage was. But after Andrew crossed south Florida, it went into the Gulf and came up into Louisiana. I was assigned to Louisiana, west of New Orleans along the coast, an area that is largely rural and very, very poor. The devastation there was terrible.

Going there allowed me to see a culture and a group of people that I otherwise would never have been involved with, and they were some of the most wonderful people. I remember going into a restaurant in New Iberia, Louisiana when somebody recognized me as a Red Cross worker and the whole restaurant broke out in applause. People came over to the table and said, "I know you're not from here, but we so much appreciate that you came as a volunteer all the way from Connecticut to help us." That kind of feeling is very hard to capture, but it really makes you *feel* good when you know that not only have you *done* good, but also you're appreciated for what you've done.

When you're working with Red Cross volunteers and employees under intense disaster conditions, you really learn to respect what they bring to the effort, and you learn not to read them by their appearance, or their background, or their education. You learn to read them by their actions. And that's a great gift that I think Red Cross gives its workers.

There are some other very practical reasons why people stay with Red Cross over time. Clearly the humanitarian thing is one, but the relationships are another. I've made a lot of friends from all walks of life. Finally, the Red Cross recognizes you—this is an organization that knows how to thank volunteers. We had a volunteer in Greenwich for many years named Cappy Crane [Mrs. Newton Crane], and Cappy used to work regularly at all the blood drives. When you'd finished donating blood, you sat in a canteen area, where you had something to eat, something to drink—until you felt completely rested and relaxed, and then you'd leave. Well, while you were at the canteen, Cappy would come over and serve deviled eggs or some other special treat she or another volunteer had made. So you were treated with a little special food. Then Cappy would give you a back rub and talk to you and say, "Oh, it was so great that you came in today," and "You've helped save somebody's life today with your donation." Wow! What a rush! You felt so good about giving.

And I think that's one of the reasons many Red Cross volunteers keep coming back—because somebody took the time to thank them for what they did, and to make them realize how special they are. I'll admit it—it feels good when somebody says, "Thank you for giving blood today," or "Thank you for helping us with this project—you really made a difference."

Ross Ogden served two back-to-back terms on the board of the Greenwich chapter from 1971 to 1977. He was chapter chairman from 1974 to 1976. He also served on the Red Cross's State Advisory Council, a group made up of representatives from various chapters around the state, and he chaired the Connecticut Disaster Committee for the Red Cross.

Ogden chaired the Northeast Regional Committee in the early 1990s, which worked with chapters in New York and New England to build their capacity to deliver services and raise funds. He went on to become the national chair of chapter services and shared responsibility with the senior vice president of the American Red Cross for all chapters in the U.S. and its territories. He appointed to the national Board of Governors in 2001, and still serves in that capacity today.

He continues to volunteer on local and national disasters. After 9/11 Ogden helped run the family support center for the eighteen families in Greenwich that had had either a direct loss or had a significant family member involved in the tragedy. Later he served as the Disaster Welfare Inquiry officer, and then as the assistant officer for administration in Connecticut. Ogden recently has completed training to join the Red Cross Critical Response Team, a leadership group designed to facilitate response to transportation accidents, mass casualty incidents and domestic terrorism. After Hurricane Katrina in 2005 Ogden spent five weeks in Mississippi as the Red Cross liaison to state and local government.

Martha Gebhardt
Whidbey Island, Washington

*M*artha Gebhardt was just a toddler during World War II, but one thing she remembers of the war years was her mother's involvement with the Red Cross. Berta Lou Gibbins Fridge volunteered as a Gray Lady in Shreveport, Louisiana, for thirty-five years. "I remember lots and lots of ladies in our home, knitting stockings and scarves and rolling bandages for the troops," recalls Gebhardt.

In 1957, when she was just seventeen, Gebhardt married and moved to Athens, Texas, where she spent more than twenty years as a housewife and the mother of three children. In 1978 the family moved to Seattle, where she became a Red Cross volunteer. "It seemed like the natural thing to do—follow in my mother's footsteps," says Gebhardt. Her first job was as chairperson of volunteer candy stripers at local hospitals.

Meanwhile, she enrolled in nursing school at Bellevue Community College outside of Seattle and graduated in 1979, just before her fortieth birthday. She took a job as a neonatal nurse in the intensive care unit, and signed on to become a Red Cross disaster volunteer. Gebhardt was able to combine her nursing expertise with her volunteer work, responding to as many as two fires a week.

Five years later she went on her first national disaster assignment after Hurricane Juan hit the Gulf Coast in November 1985. Her marriage was falling apart, and it was on such an assignment that she met fellow Red Cross volunteer, Mel Gebhardt. They later married. Together the couple has traveled the country doing disaster work, first as volunteers and later as paid staff "reservists," on call for national disasters.

Gebhardt's Red Cross career has taken her on some seventy-five disasters, a number matched by only a handful of her peers. "I've been on assignment *with Red Cross from the Virgin Islands to Guam and about everywhere in between," she says. "Tornadoes, earthquakes, fires, floods, planes crashes, the World Trade Center—you name it, I've been there."*

When Hurricane Juan hit Louisiana in 1985, the Red Cross was desperate for volunteers because it was the third big storm in three months. The Seattle chapter called me and asked if I wanted to go. I had wanted to go out on my first national disaster, and I had already taken the classes now known as Disaster Health One and Two, so I said, "Sure, I'll go."

My first assignment was working for the health services officer at chapter headquarters in New Orleans. Essentially, we drove around to the various shelters and service centers to see what families' needs and problems were. After about three days, my supervisor told me, "Go do it yourself—you know what you're doing." So I spent ten days doing that, then I worked in two different service centers in an area southeast of New Orleans.

We provide emergency relief. Our role is as an advocate for the client. If they're sick and it's disaster-related, we provide necessary medica-

COURTESY OF THE AUSTIN AMERICAN-STATESMAN
Mel and Martha Gebhardt on assignment in Texas, 1997

tions and send them to the doctor. When there is a fatality, we help with funerals, funeral clothes and counseling. If there are other people in the family that were injured and are in the hospital, we help them work out how they are going to pay the bills and facilitate getting them on Medicaid or whatever they need to do to get their bills paid. Our main goal is to get clients back into their own healthcare system, where they can get the follow-up care they need, whether it's physical or mental.

On a day-to-day basis, our job is replacing medications that get wet, mostly blood pressure or heart medications. We also replace glasses and dentures that are damaged, as well as wheelchairs, hospital beds and even prostheses—I've helped replace artificial legs, arms, even eyes. For example, we get in touch with one of the support groups for blind people, and they lead us to medical resources. If the client doesn't have insurance, we work something out with the support group, or a foundation that can help.

On that first disaster, I stayed in Louisiana for three weeks. The work was just so exhilarating. It seems odd to say it this way, but I fell in love with disaster work. Every time they called for additional staffing, I'd volunteer. I went to the February flood near Reva City, California, the next year. I was working for an agency doing neonatal intensive care nursing in various Seattle hospitals so I could set my own hours—and volunteer when I wanted to. There are so many times where you're in situations where something terrible happens and you say, "Oh, I wish I could do something, but I don't know what." Well, with Red Cross, there's always something you can do.

Then in September 1988, I was sent to forest fires near Sacramento, California. They were called the "Forty-nine Fires"—they affected two hundred counties. It was Mel's first national disaster. He was a police officer, a superintendent for the youth conservation corps in California, and he had recently retired in 1985. On this job he was the ERV driver, and I met him when he pulled up his ERV at the service center. It was my first day on the job, September 21st, and it was my forty-ninth birthday.

Mel had lived in California all his life, and I lived in Washington, but the next year, we met again on the Central American Refugee situation in Brownsville, Texas. In between the disasters, we didn't see each other, but we talked fairly frequently on the phone, about once a week. I had just gotten divorced, and I just considered him a friend.

Finally we went to Hurricane Hugo together in Puerto Rico. I was on the first commercial flight in after Hugo hit Puerto Rico on September 17, 1989. Mel was on the second plane—he arrived about an hour behind me. Where the hurricane hit, it was total devastation. The trees were all either down or stripped. About nine hundred people were stranded and completely surrounded by water—on what had become an island. We had to take a boat to check on them.

We had one client whose home was surrounded by water. She was an elderly woman, a widow, and she lived in a typical house, which is tin and wood pieces kind of strung together. Her roof had been blown off. Some people were living under her front porch. The first time we went there, the National Guard took us out there. We set up a boating system where we could get food and water to her on a regular basis. We also provided her with blood pressure medication.

When the Red Cross comes to the scene of a disaster, it's with an integrated care program—where family services, health services, mental health, mass care all work together on a family's situation to provide whatever's needed. For example, there may be a pocket of clients out in the field who have not been seen; mass care will bring their contact information or location to us. We share that information with family services, and then a team goes out there and takes care of their needs, whether it's running a feeding route into that area, or making sure their health services needs are met, or they've got clothes and a place to stay. And I think working together like that, and working the long, hard hours we do—usually twelve, fourteen, fifteen hours for six days a week, brings you close to the people you're working with. When the Loma Prieta earthquake happened in San Francisco in October 1989, less than a month after Hugo hit, Mel and I both stayed behind for three months—so much was needed for the recovery effort. And that's when we fell in love and decided to get married. He gave me a "remembrance" ring, an opal, on a deserted beach one afternoon.

A few months later, Mel came up to Seattle to live, and we got married at the St. Bernard's Visitor Center on Mt. Rainier on August 11, 1990. There were about thirty-five Red Cross friends there. They all got together and gave us our wedding gift, a hot air balloon ride, which we took on our first anniversary.

Since then, we've pretty much gone on disaster assignments together. We've done tornadoes and hurricanes in Florida, floods in Mississippi and Louisiana, hurricanes in Louisiana, tornadoes in Kentucky, tornadoes in Minnesota, floods in Detroit, a tornado in Albany, New York, and ice storms in Maine. I've been to North Carolina after hurricanes so many times—five years in a row from 1999 to 2003—I think I know almost everybody in that state. And we were both assigned to New York at the same time for eight weeks after 9/11.

We since have both retired from active disaster work. I miss the camaraderie with all my Red Cross friends—we worked long, hard hours but we also made some great friends. Of course, we stay in touch by e-mail as they are all over the place—from Guam to Puerto Rico.

We always had our bags packed, ready to go with two to three weeks worth of clothes. And we also had all we needed to start up a job in another bag—all the Red Cross disaster forms and supplies like pens and pencils, rulers and staplers. We had the mail stopped and my daughter would go through it two to three times a month. Most of our bills were automatically arranged through the bank, but she had our checkbook if something needed to be paid.

We could almost plan our year by the disaster calendar. We pretty much gauged what we might be doing by the time of year. March, April, May, and sometimes February and June, are the tornado months. The summers are wildfires, or if they've had a lot of rain in an area where they've had wildfires before, they could possibly flood, because there's no grass to hold the water. Of course, that's also hurricane season, from June to November, but we don't really look for those until later on in September and October. Then you've got floods in November, December and January. Of course, there's always the unexpected—like a plane crash.

One job that gave me a lot of satisfaction was in Jerrell, Texas.

It's just out of Austin, and it has maybe a thousand people. It got hit by an F5 tornado, a big huge one, in May, 1997. The tornado hit a subdivision and the whole area was completely flat—even the streets were rolled up. Before the tornado, it was a middle class area with trees and fences. But it was all gone, bare.

Thirty people were killed. I remember one family in particular—a family of five that were big churchgoers and did a lot for the community, and they were all killed. The town was devastated. I was the Red Cross health services officer, and Mel was a mass care officer. We did all the usual, replacing medications and tending to medical needs. That kind of thing.

The state pitched in with funds funneled through the Red Cross. We were actually able to write checks for all the funeral expenses, the health and hospital bills, and we usually didn't get to do that. One of my jobs was to deliver the checks to the families in need. That was *extremely* satisfying. Of course, I was just the messenger bringing help and hope, but being able to do that for that community really makes you feel awfully good.

Of course, New York after 9/11 was unforgettable. I was an assistant officer in New York on two different occasions. My job was mostly at headquarters, staffing and dealing with problems that came up, whether it concerned supplies, or nurses who were unhappy with their assignments, because every single one of them wanted to work at Ground Zero in the residence centers. Mel was the mass care officer in charge of feeding in the residence centers.

One of my most memorable experiences occurred during the memorial service for family members of the victims at Ground Zero. This was before they built the big ramp down into the pit, so it was early on, about four or five weeks into the job. Very few of the family members had been to Ground Zero at that point, so for most, this was their first visit. We had nursing and mental health staff as escorts for the families. A fair amount of the rubble had already been cleared, and the memorial service was held right on the street, in front of Building Two. The World Trade Center was still smoking, and the hoses sprayed water on it the whole time we were there. My husband

and I were both down there, and he was serving hot chocolate and coffee.

It was very cold and very windy, and we got down there about 10 A.M., and the service didn't start until 2:00. We were setting up things and getting ready, looking after our staff, and then the families began to arrive by buses. The thinking was that two thousand people would attend; nine thousand showed up.

Mental health workers were on each bus, escorting families in, and then we met them as they got off of the buses. I probably escorted between thirty and fifty people that day. But this one lady really struck me—she was so devastated. You could see it on her face—it radiated from her. And I went over and took her hand, and I said, "Would you like me to take you to your seat?" She said, "Sure," and we started walking into Ground Zero, which was a couple streets away from where the buses let them off. And when we turned the corner and she saw the devastation up close, she kept repeating, "Oh, my love, my love, what have they done to you?"

And it was all I could do to keep from crying. I couldn't do that—I wouldn't have been any help to her if I'd started bawling. I needed to remain professional. So I just held onto her hand a little tighter, and I held onto her arm to steady her. When we got to her seat, she wouldn't let go for a little while, so I just stood there and held her hand until she was ready to release it. Then I said, "I'm going to step back and I'll be right here if you need me." And she said, "Thank you very much." That was the last I ever spoke to her. She was in her late thirties, early forties, a very tall, well-groomed, elegant lady. I don't know anything else about her other than she lost her husband. I don't know her name, I have no earthly idea where she was from, not a thing. But she will stay with me for the rest of my life.

Mel Gebhardt retired from Red Cross disaster relief work in 2003 and Martha retired in September 2004. The following January, Martha suffered two back-to-back strokes. She is recuperating at her home in a house the couple built on Whidbey Island, Washington.

Warren Zorek
New York, New York

---

*J*ust *before World War II broke out, some ten thousand Jewish children were sent to England for sanctuary through a program known as Kindertransport. Warren "Winnie" Zorek was one of them. When Zorek was twelve years old, his parents put him on a train to England. They never saw one another again. Zorek's parents, his fourteen-year-old sister, and dozens of other relatives stayed behind in Germany.*

However, Zorek was able to correspond with his parents via the International Committee of the Red Cross, even after they no longer lived in their home. In 1959, after he made his way to New York City, married and began a successful career in retail, Zorek became a Red Cross volunteer as a way of expressing his gratitude.

Over the next four decades, he volunteered his time and energy at every major disaster and innumerable fires in New York City. He also served as disaster chairman for the American Red Cross in Greater New York for more than two decades until he stepped down in 2000. When he retired from his job as a merchandising manager for Bloomingdale's Department Store in 1992, Zorek spent much of his free time on national disaster assignments.

In 1990, Zorek became involved with an incipient Red Cross program in New York called Project Search, the New York branch of the newly formed American Red Cross Holocaust and War Victims Tracing and Information Center in Baltimore. After witnessing several reunions, in 2002 Zorek finally decided to find out the fate of the fifty-eight members of his own family lost in the Holocaust—relatives he believed had been dead for some sixty years.

I was born in 1925 in Breslau, which was Germany at the time. It became part of Poland after the war. I had a normal life and a wonderful family. As a child, I was unaware of the problems of the Jewish people. I really never experienced any difficulties.

Then in 1937, my parents put me on a train with other children to send me to a camp in Dovercourt, England, a city on the coast southeast of London. It was a Butlins holiday camp—a place people would go for a week or weekend on vacation. We slept in little one-room buildings and we went to a big mess hall for meals and meetings. I thought it was a wonderful place—to me it was a great adventure. A lot of children from Germany and Austria were there. The Austrians sang a song called "Vienna, City of My Dreams." Whenever they started playing it, all of the kids cried.

I lived there for about a year. Next, some of us went to a place called Clayton near the east coast of England near Ipswich. It was an old residence owned by an English lord. We slept in big rooms with bunk beds. I was there a few months.

About the time the war broke out in 1939, I went to live in a

COURTESY OF THE AMERICAN RED CROSS

Warren Zorek in front of the World Trade Center after the 1993 bombing

foster home in Gloucester, a town on River Severn on the west coast of England that adopted ten or twelve children. When the sirens warning of an air raid went off, school started a couple of hours late. So my classmates and I would say to one another, "We'll meet you at a specific place like a garage behind someone's home, a half hour after the sirens go off." It was quite an adventure.

At school I met a boy named Jim Thew and he invited me to tea with his parents and three brothers. They decided to take in a poor Jewish boy. They asked me to come live with them so I left the foster home and lived with the family about four or five years. They were wonderful people.

Until the war broke out, I communicated with my parents using normal mail between England and Germany. But once the war began, the only way my parents and I could correspond was through the Red Cross. My parents would send a double-paged hand-written letter addressed to me to the Red Cross in Switzerland. The Red Cross would forward it to England. I would write a note on the back of the letter and mail it back to Switzerland, and the Swiss Red Cross would send it back to Germany. My parents mostly wrote about family things—this aunt is going here, and this cousin was doing that. I'm sure there was more to it than I could understand. I remember one letter my parents sent while I was at camp in Dovercourt. They tried to explain that I should be very careful of older men. I'll always remember that—but I didn't understand it at the time.

This went on until 1942. The letters stopped coming. Of course, at the time I did not realize they stopped. I never heard from any of them again. I never got any facts about what happened to my family, but I think they were sent to Auschwitz. I had a sister named Erna who was two years older than I was. She stayed with my parents, and she was part of my family that was lost.

I came to the United States after the war ended in 1947. I was twenty-one years old. I had a cousin in New York in the tobacco business, and so at first I worked in his shop on 87th Street and Third Avenue—it just happened to be two blocks away from where I live now on 86th Street and Madison Avenue.

I married Jane Popper in 1956. Her father, Edward Popper, had been unable to serve in the army, so he became a volunteer with the New York City Fire Department in his spare time. At the time, the fire department had a canteen—a fire department employee would drive it to the scene and volunteers like my father-in-law would make coffee when it was cold and lemonade in warm weather for the firemen. They called themselves the Third Alarm Association. I started volunteering with them in 1959. When the city was short of funds in the 1970s the first thing to go was the fire-department canteen. The Red Cross stepped up and provided both the canteen and the volunteers to staff it at fires and other disasters, as well as doing their traditional role of taking care of victims.

At the time, the Bronx was burning up—there were fires every day, nearly twenty-four hours a day. You could go up to the Bronx any time of night and you could be sure to find a fire. It was like a cancer. Vagrants started a fire in one part of a building to keep warm and the fire department would put it out. The next day there'd be another fire in another part of the same building.

I have always gotten a lot of satisfaction out of being able to help people that need help, people that appreciate receiving help. There are so many different ways of helping—it's not just giving them a cup of lemonade or coffee. I remember one time a family was burned out, and through the Red Cross, I helped people put a deposit on their rent and down payment on some furniture. The Red Cross doesn't do that anymore. Today, the city does that, or FEMA, on national disasters.

We also used to take families out shopping for clothing and the Red Cross paid for it. One time there was a fire on 52nd Street and Third Avenue, and everyone who lived in the building had to be evacuated. There were about forty-five to fifty people, and they had nothing left, just blankets and coats. I was working at Bloomingdale's then, and I had arranged for the store to open early. We took them up there and the families did their own shopping. We opened at 7:00 that morning for them, and by 9:00 they all had new clothes.

One of the worst fires I can recall was the Happy Land Social Club fire. It happened on Sunday, March 25, 1990. I had the fire radio on at home and I heard the dispatcher say that there were eighty-seven DOAs. I couldn't believe it. Most of the victims were from Honduras. We set up the disaster relief operation in a school across the street from the fire scene.

The Red Cross was in charge of transporting the victims' bodies to Honduras for burial and arranging for their families to attend the services. Although the army was going to initially transport the bodies back to Honduras, the state department decided it wasn't the right thing for the military to be involved in, and so the Red Cross chartered a plane. To make the caskets fit, we had to stack them, but we quickly learned that you can't stack a casket because the lid isn't flat. Between Friday and Saturday, we got three firms in Brooklyn to make a wood shelf with a flat surface for forty-eight caskets plus two spaces for flowers. Also, since it was a small plane it wasn't pressurized. We had to open all of the caskets because there couldn't be a vacuum or the caskets would pop open. So we unscrewed the lids. These are among the many, many things I learned from the Red Cross.

In addition to fires, there were also a lot of other big local disasters over the years. I worked a building collapse in Times Square, the Fourteenth Street subway crash and a fire at the Blue Angel Nightclub. I was out at Kennedy Airport in 1988 after the explosion of Pan Am Flight 103 over Lockerbie, Scotland, because so many relatives were arriving at Kennedy, and again in January 1990 after an Avianca plane crashed near Kennedy. I also helped after a U.S. Air flight crashed on takeoff at La Guardia Airport in 1992. Of course, there was also the first World Trade Center bombing in 1993.

That was mostly a feeding operation and taking care of the people who worked in the building. It was a Friday afternoon and we helped the Hasidic Jews who worked there get home. They weren't allowed to take the subway or get in a car on the Sabbath. When we called their homes nobody would pick up the phone. We handled each case separately. Some ended up staying in a hotel overnight and others walked home over the Brooklyn Bridge.

After I retired from my job at Bloomingdale's in 1992, I went to one disaster after another in the next few years—Florida after Hurricane Andrew that year, Los Angeles after the 1994 earthquake, West Virginia and California after floods in 1995, Minnesota and North Dakota after floods in 1997, and St. Louis after floods in 1998.

I did several different functions on a national disaster. After Hurricane Andrew I worked in a warehouse. After the earthquake in Los Angeles, I opened a family service center in Northridge and I stayed there for three to four weeks. We handled nearly two hundred people a day.

Soon I got involved with the "Gifts In Kind" program on national disasters. Instead of asking for a cash donation, the Red Cross asks manufacturers and suppliers directly for the kind of aid—food, blankets, whatever—it needs. Because of my work experience at Bloomingdale's as a marketing manager, I knew how to get this done. After TWA Flight 800 crashed in 1997, I went out to Kennedy Airport as soon as I heard about it, right after it happened. I was there all day. I went home to get some sleep and I got a call asking me to go back out to Long Island because the staff and victim's families needed food.

Before I left, I made a call to Kraft Foods. I told them what we needed and that it would be a long-term operation. I started driving out to the island and by the time I got there, two trucks of food were already on the way. I arrived at 2:00 in the morning and they unloaded snacks, soft drinks and all sorts of stuff. We worked with Kraft Foods on pretty much every major disaster so they knew what to send. I stayed out there for four weeks. I remember one unusual request on that assignment: There were several divers on the search and rescue teams and they requested playing cards. They played cards on breaks. You get all sorts of requests.

On September 11th, I went to the chapter as soon as I heard that a plane had hit the World Trade Center. My job was working on "Gifts In Kind." The first thing they needed was plastic Ziploc bags. All food had to be in Ziploc bags because they didn't know what kind of contaminants were down there. So I found out who makes Ziploc bags, Johnson and Son, Inc. out of Wisconsin. I called them up and they sent a truckload of Ziploc bags—we still have boxes of them. All told, I brought in over five million dollars worth of goods. Food and bottled water is always important. So are phone cards—they are useful for both volunteers and victims.

After 9/11, I worked at the Greater New York chapter first, then they moved the main operation to the Brooklyn chapter in Brooklyn Heights, where I spent ninety days. I would go at 6:00 in the morning every day. That was my last national job.

Another thing I did with the Red Cross—probably because of my own background in the war—I got involved with Project Search, which traces people who have become separated from their families as a result of war. This really got started after the former Soviet Union opened its war archives in 1989 and turned over their records to the International Red Cross. Suddenly, millions of documents became available. The American Red Cross started a separate operation headquartered in Baltimore, the Holocaust and War Victims Tracing and Information Center. I became the New York representative, and served as chairman for three years. All told, the center has reunited more than a thousand people.

There are many, many ways of finding people. It's not easy. It's very time consuming. First, we learn as much as we can about the family and those who are missing—names, birth dates, where they lived. Then you look for immigration papers, driver's licenses, and marriage and death certificates.

I didn't bother to try and trace my family because it seemed futile. I thought everyone in my family had died. My mother was one of seven children so there's seven right there, and most of them were married. There were fifty-eight relatives in all from both my mother's and father's sides of the family whom I never heard from after the war.

But after witnessing two reunions, I realized I wanted to find out what happened to my own family. Somebody in Philadelphia was looking for their relatives named Werner—the same name of several people in my mother's family. We called them and it wasn't a match for the person I was helping, but the volunteer at the Red Cross in Philadelphia said, "Maybe it's a relative of yours."

She was right. It was my second cousin, Werner Freund. Werner's father, George, was one of my mother's seven siblings. It happened so fast. When I found out he was alive, I picked up the phone and called Brazil where he lives. We spoke English—my German isn't very good. I learned that when the rest of our family was taken from their homes, he survived because he was on vacation in Italy. He had called a friend of his in Germany who said, "Don't ever come back."

COURTESY OF WARREN ZOREK

Warren Zorek and his older cousin George in Germany

It turned out Werner has a brother in Israel, Amit. So I called Israel. Werner is ninety years old. Werner's son, George, who also lives in Brazil, works for a company that also has offices in New York. He comes up here once in awhile and that's how we met. I've been in touch with them since then by e-mail.

After 9/11 I began to create a family tree on the computer of all of my family members who died in the Holocaust. My wife, two children, three grandchildren and I were the only living relatives listed. Once I found out about my cousins who survived, I filled in their names, and the names of more than twenty new relatives—including children and grandchildren. My fourth grandchild will be added to the family tree soon.

The hallway of Warren Zorek's New York apartment is lined with framed disaster plaques and many local and national volunteer awards. He received Bess Kaufman Outstanding Volunteer Award from Red Cross national headquarters in 2000, and the American Red Cross in Greater New York Volunteer of the Year Award in 1991 and 1992. He was chairman of Red Cross events for Liberty Weekend, the nation's centennial in 1976 and a former member of the board of directors of the New York chapter.

After working on Project Search in a variety of capacities, Zorek retired as chairman in 2001. He remains active in his synagogue, and in other community organizations. In 1996 he was one of twenty-eight New Yorkers selected to carry the Olympic torch through New York.

At age 80, Zorek rarely goes to disasters in the middle of the night. But he still keeps his fire department radio on all night.

Chapter 4

RED, WHITE AND BLUE:
Disaster Relief in the New Century

The city, for the first time in its long history, is destructible. A single flight of planes no bigger than a wedge of geese can quickly end this island fantasy, burn the towers, crumble the bridges, turn the underground passages into lethal chambers, cremate the millions. The intimation of mortality is part of New York now; in the sounds of jets overhead, in the black headlines of the latest editions.

— E.B. White, *Here Is New York,* 1949

On the morning of September 11, 2001, millions of Americans stared at their TV sets after two hijacked planes struck the World Trade Center. While most Americans were virtually immobilized by the tragedy unfolding on live television, thousands of Red Cross volunteers and staff sprang into action.

In New York, teams of Red Cross disaster workers raced downtown. One ERV was at the scene before the South Tower collapsed and was parked so close when it happened that debris from the building crashed onto the truck. By nightfall Red Cross staff had opened thirteen shelters in New York City, and across the river in New Jersey, several more shelters housed thousands of people unable to get back to their homes in New York.

Around the country hundreds of other Red Cross chapters sprang into action. Within hours after the Twin Towers and the Pentagon were hit, staff and volunteers loaded trucks with supplies and got on the road themselves to spend weeks assisting with the relief operation. The American Red Cross of Greater Idaho in Boise alone sent seventy-four people. They came from every state, and other countries, an army of 55,000 Red Crossers in all.

Within a week the disaster relief operation was in full swing. The family assistance center at Pier 94 on the Hudson River served as a hub for the families of the close to three thousand missing people. More than a dozen Red Cross service centers were up and running around the city. Respite centers were an oasis for rescue workers, with food available twenty-four hours a day, and nurses, mental health professionals and even massage therapists on hand. Spiritual counselors representing all faiths made themselves available for disaster victims, the families of the missing, and relief workers. Similar centers were set up near the Pentagon in Virginia, where a third passenger jet struck the building, and in Shanksville, Pennsylvania, where another hijacked plane crashed.

Regardless of where they worked, Red Crossers found the experience disconcerting. Lisa Arhontes, who oversaw the feeding operation at Saint John's Respite Center, recalls that simply being at Ground Zero was intense. "If a body or any remains were discovered, there was an unusual sound that would go off and we would

COURTESY OF THE
AMERICAN RED CROSS

**Red Cross workers in New York after
September 11, 2001**

all stand outside to bear witness," she says. "We realized that we were very close to something profound." For months the Red Cross stayed on the scene, offering food round-the-clock to families and workers, counseling to the firemen and other workers who had the depressing task of sifting through the carnage, as well as to the families of those who lost loved ones. It was an enormous undertaking.

Donations poured in at a record pace. Bob Bender, at the time CEO of the American Red Cross in Greater New York, literally had people stuffing money in the pockets of his Red Cross jacket while he walked the streets of the city. From lemonade stands to car washes to celebrity telethons, it seemed as though everyone was doing his or her part.

But within weeks the Red Cross was embroiled in a controversy that threatened to overshadow the immense relief operation. The organization came under fire—not only from the families of those affected, but also from the media and Congress—for attempting to divert $264 million in 9/11 donations to a corporate nest egg intended for future terror attacks. Other criticisms were that the Red Cross dispersed cash assistance too slowly and did not cooperate with other relief agencies. In addition, Dr. Bernadine Healy, then president of the American Red Cross, issued urgent pleas for blood for those injured in the attacks that, as it turned out, was not needed. People in cities nationwide had stood in lines waiting to donate blood. Congressional auditors later determined that blood banks threw out more than 200,000 units of blood after 9/11. All in all, the reputation of the Red Cross suffered its worst blow in decades.

The series of crises after 9/11 came as a surprise to many Americans. But it wasn't the first time the Red Cross's problems have been brought to light because of a disaster. After the 1989 Loma Prieta earthquake in California, and the Oklahoma City bombing in 1995, Red Cross

COURTESY OF THE AMERICAN RED CROSS
Ground Zero, 2001

fundraising practices also were roundly criticized—and an oft-cited complaint was that all of the donated funds were not spent locally.

Fortunately, the public doesn't stay angry with the Red Cross for long. "The organization has amazing volunteers who have this spirit of helping, and that comes through in the eyes and hearts of the public," observes Harold Brooks, CEO of the Bay Area chapter in San Francisco. "They see what we do and will forgive us for momentary lapses."

Besides, most staff see their work as separate from whatever gaffes national headquarters might make. Mental health worker Virginia Stern explains: "As long as the problems in Washington don't interfere with the ability of the people who want to serve, and the organization continues to provide a forum for that, that's all that matters to me. Whatever went on with the administration of the Red Cross after 9/11, the people who provided services were able to do really good work."

By November of 2001 the agency had shifted gears and earmarked the funds raised in the aftermath of 9/11 solely for the victims and families of that tragedy. Healy resigned, albeit reluctantly, and former Senate majority leader George Mitchell was brought in to develop and implement a plan to allocate the $1.1 billion that came to be known as the American Red Cross Liberty Disaster Relief Fund. Within months, the Liberty Fund was folded into the September 11 Recovery Program (SRP), designed to provide both immediate and long-term assistance to the fifty-seven thousand individuals and families of those killed and seriously injured, along with workers, residents and emergency personnel who were affected by the attacks.

A large chunk of the money was set aside for mental health and substance-abuse programs, therapy and counseling that is still going strong four years later. A surge of clients arrived in the first few months after 9/11, but people have kept coming as problems emerged months—even years—later. As we go to press in December 2005 more than eleven thousand people remain enrolled in the program. Two hundred new clients continue to sign up each month.

In addition, $388 million of the Liberty Fund was allocated for direct financial assistance. The beneficiaries of those who died received $97,000 on average—far more than the victims of any previous disaster. "It was a blessing because it enabled the Red Cross to address the needs of people, but it was a curse because so many of the people impacted—where there was loss of life or injury—would focus on the money rather than taking care of their own recovery," says Alan Goodman, director of the SRP. "Families who lost loved ones in 9/11 didn't start the healing process until the money stopped flowing—only then were they able to deal with the emotional impact of the disaster."

Meanwhile, the Red Cross was also on the mend. Under the watch of a new president, Marty Evans, the charity made an honest attempt to learn from its mistakes in an effort to win back the public trust. Board of Governors member Dr. Susan Hassmiller explains some of the changes instituted after 9/11: "We're much more customer-focused, customer-friendly and more efficient." Instead of issuing vouchers as the organization did in the past, it now hands out "client assistance cards"—debit cards for necessities like food and clothing—to make it easier to receive aid.

Responding to criticism that it did not coordinate with other relief agencies in the past, the organization became more pliable when offering services alongside other agencies. To this end, the Red Cross helped create the Coordinated Assistance Network, a computerized system that enables disaster agencies to synchronize services with other agencies as well as share information about clients—with their permission. "We are not "just one cog in the wheel," as Jane Morgan, director of individual assistance says. "We're a proactive partner now, and we realize that these other agencies aren't just sub-contractors to the Red Cross."

In retrospect, the changes were necessary if the organization was to restore its name and meet the needs of the post 9/11 world, where natural disasters are inevitable and terror attacks a distinct possibility. As proof of the government's reliance on the Red Cross, the U.S. Department of Homeland Security's 2005 National Response Plan designated the Red Cross as the agency responsible for mass care, which includes providing emergency food and shelter after a disaster.* With its "Together, We Prepare" campaign, the organization again worked with Homeland Security to ready Americans for unexpected emergencies of all kinds. The initiative urges Americans to take five

---

* The role of the Federal Emergency Management Agency is to manage the federal response and recovery efforts following a disaster.

simple steps—make a plan, build a kit, get trained, give blood and volunteer. In doing so, the Red Cross proved once again that it is not only resilient, but relevant. "The Red Cross continually reinvents itself," says Ken Curtin, former Red Cross disaster services director in New York City, who currently is FEMA's (Federal Emergency Management Agency) liaison to voluntary agencies, including the Red Cross.

Despite these changes, the goal of the Red Cross on the scene of any disaster remains the same: to meet the needs of those affected as quickly as possible. In addition to providing food and shelter for disaster victims, services range from replacing lost medicine to providing for a new mattress or pair of shoes. "There are a lot of people out there who think the Red Cross is just sandwiches and drinks," says Peter Teahen, a Red Cross volunteer from Cedar Rapids, Iowa. "They don't understand the breadth of services offered by the organization." Mental health counseling, for instance, was added to the list in 1989 after Hurricane Hugo, and today the Red Cross is the agency responsible for ensuring that psychologists and other mental health providers are available following domestic disasters.

While the organization was restoring its good name, it faced another set of challenges in the first years of the new century. A faltering economy, donor fatigue after 9/11, and a succession of costly natural disasters, including massive wildfires in California and a few active hurricane seasons, emptied its coffers. Services had to be cut back. As a result, longtime Red Crossers were understandably upset. Martha Gebhardt, a nurse from Whidbey Island, Washington, complains that the Red Cross no longer provides the depth of services at the scene of a disaster as it had in the past. Gebhardt lamented when she worked in Virginia after Hurricane Isabel in 2003, for instance, that funding per client was half of what it once was, $500 instead of $1,000, and the dispensing of expensive medications was severely curtailed. "It hurt not to be able to do what we thought we should be doing for clients," she says. "We didn't feel like we had done our job."

The disaster relief fund had been running on empty for more than a year when the first of four consecutive hurricanes battered Florida and other parts of the Gulf Coast in August 2004. Despite the lack of funds, the Red Cross managed to do what it does every time a disaster occurs—it dispatched staff, supplies and vehicles from all over the country to the scene within hours. "It's like watching a multi-million dollar business open overnight," says Jean Jacob, a longtime volunteer from San Francisco who worked in Florida after one of the 2004 hurricanes. Before the hurricane season was over that year, the Red Cross had served ten million meals, set up 1,733 shelters and housed 415,589 people. But the storms' toll was so high the Red Cross required a federal government bailout to foot the bill.

It was obvious that the agency had become more accountable shortly after the tsunami hit Asia on December 26, 2004. The American Red Cross raised $535 million* and outlined a plan to show how it would spend the money. Then Evans announced that enough money had been raised to pay for the relief operation. "We intend to do this whenever we can see the end of the need for a particular disaster on the horizon," she says. Her announcement was a welcome change from the past, and helped restore the public's confidence in the Red Cross.

Then came Katrina. Both the federal government and the Red Cross were overwhelmed after this massive category four hurricane came ashore on August 29 in Louisiana, Mississippi and Alabama. More than

Courtesy of Gene Dailey

Red Cross distribution site in Slidell, Louisiana after Hurricane Katrina, 2005

---

* $1.2 billion was pledged to Red Cross societies worldwide.

a thousand people died in those two states, and whole towns were wiped off the map in a ninety-thousand square mile swath of destruction.

In New Orleans, Katrina's effects were catastrophic. Three-fourths of the city was underwater after rising waters breached the levees. Kay Wilkins, CEO of the Southeast Louisiana chapter of the American Red Cross in New Orleans, says that the storm took a huge toll on her chapter as well. All but one of the twelve service delivery centers suffered damage in their parishes from Katrina or Hurricane Rita, which hit just weeks later. The chapter, located on Canal Street, had four to six feet of water and remained uninhabitable for months. In addition, thirty percent of Wilkins' staff left town. "My disaster director resigned and my leadership was pretty much broke," she says. "We are still trying to find our other disaster volunteers. We had 900 before the storm—but we've only found about fifty—less than ten percent."

Wilkins, who has been with the chapter for twenty-five years, was left with about forty staff and volunteers who headed north just before the storm and have been working ever since. "The volunteers and staff who stayed pre- and post-Katrina are some of the heroes of the storm," says Wilkins. "They had great courage." Fifteen of those people had homes that were destroyed, yet they continued to work on the disaster relief operation. Some lived in staff shelters until December and then moved into hotels, where they remained at Christmas, four months after Katrina decimated their city.

When volunteers and visiting staff began to show up a few days after the storm, Wilkins hugged as many as she could and thanked them for coming and relieving some of the local staff. Tom Stark of Riverside, Connecticut, was one of the first volunteers on the scene. He was stationed in Covington, Louisiana, on the north side of Lake Pontchartrain in a supervisory role in mass care. Stark was responsible for six hundred staff, twenty-one shelters, twenty-nine ERVs and five mobile kitchens that served eighteen thousand meals a day. "It took ten days to turn this around to the point that things were getting better not worse, but that speaks to the magnitude of the disaster," says Stark. The response was the largest ever to a natural disaster in the history of the American Red Cross, and in the middle of it, Hurricane

Rita bore down on the Gulf Coast. Now a million Texans needed to be evacuated to higher ground. The Red Cross again set up shelters in advance of the storm—in some cases in some towns in Texas, where Katrina evacuees were still living.

The need after Katrina in 2005 dwarfed the response to the four hurricanes the year before. The Red Cross staffed more than a thousand shelters in twenty-seven states, housing a record 118,000 evacuees in one night. By November the Red Cross, in conjunction with the Southern Baptist Convention, had served twenty-five million hot meals. With the help of FEMA, the Red Cross rolled out a new program to arrange for hotels for those left homeless. And they began helping to find the thousands of missing children who had been separated from their families. An elaborate communications network, including a phone system and Internet kiosks, was created to enable shelter residents to locate relatives who might be lost or were missing.

An enormous fundraising campaign kicked in to support the colossal relief effort. Supermarket checkouts, ATMs, and numerous Web sites solicited money. Even Major League Baseball batting helmets were emblazoned with the Red Cross symbol. Kids set up lemonade stands. School children pitched in with their allowances. Men turned over their winnings from Friday night poker tournaments. Celebrities and socialites attending a horse show in the Hamptons on Long Island, New York, lined up at a Red Cross booth collecting donations.

This time "donor intent" was the buzzword, and if you wanted your money to go for Katrina relief, that's how it was spent. The Red Cross also saw to it that the cash got into the hands of those who needed it quickly. The agency set up an 800 number—another first— where people could call to get cash-assistance cards, cash, vouchers and checks. At three call centers in California, New York and Virginia, the staff fielded a million calls every twenty-four hours. More than two million people representing 721,000 households received cash assistance amounting to a thousand dollars on average. At the height of the disaster relief operation in September, the Red Cross reported that it was spending $35 million a day on financial assistance alone, and the agency predicted that simply meeting emergency needs of Katrina and Rita victims would cost over $2 billion. The organization ended up taking out a $364 million loan to cover the disaster relief operation until more money is donated.

How did the Red Cross stack up this time around? While FEMA, state and local governments were scorned for the inadequate, slow response to the disaster early on, criticisms of the Red Cross dimmed in comparison. The agency took the lion's share of donated funds and therefore there were questions about how the money was being spent, but they were answered head on. "Since 9/11 we can trace a donated dollar from the point of donation to expenditure," explains Paige Roberts, CEO of the Southeastern Mississippi chapter of the Red Cross. "Some people think we're taking all the money, but whatever money we raise, we need."

A few months after the storm grievances began to mount. In addition to providing an inaccurate tally of evacuees living in hotels, the Red Cross fielded complaints about the red tape in applying for assistance, the long waits in getting through to the hotlines, uneven assistance in different geographical areas, and inequities in the treatment of racial groups. But given the scope of the disaster, many people continue to commend the Red Cross performance. "It was a real Red Cross success story," says Stark, who was on the scene in Louisiana for more than two weeks.

Paige Roberts agrees that the organization is to be lauded for its overall response to Katrina, but she refers to the agency as "the eight hundred pound gorilla" when it comes to disaster relief agencies. "Considering the magnitude of this disaster, the American Red Cross has a lot to be proud of," she says. "But an organization that's been in the business for that long should be one of, if not the best, responder."

Katrina's legacy to the Red Cross is that the response may amount to the largest mobilization of Americans working as volunteers since WWII. Most had no prior contact with the Red Cross. Many of the new recruits will go home and sign up with their local chapters so they can join the ranks of those called upon to volunteer in time for next year's hurricane season. As Melvin Reeves, assistant director of the September 11 Recovery Program in New York, likes to say, "People *become* the Red Cross in an emergency."

Virginia Stern
New York, New York

After working as a social worker in private practice for thirty years, Virginia Stern signed up for a Red Cross disaster services course in July 2001. Her first assignment came three months later on September 11th, when disaster struck in her own backyard. Stern has lived in New York City's East Village for thirty-five years, and from the corner by her apartment, she could see the World Trade Center. In the days and weeks after 9/11, Stern volunteered night and day at various locations throughout New York City.

When she told the Red Cross that she was willing to "give three days a week to this effort for as long as it takes," Stern was informed of the three-week limit on national disaster assignments. She ignored it, and so did the Red Cross. "I called every week and said, 'I can come in Monday, Tuesday and Wednesday,'" recalls Stern. "After a while, I was just penciled in."

Stern spent three days a week at Ground Zero for ten months and she continued to volunteer one day a week at the September 11 Recovery Program until March 2004. "I felt very strongly that since it was my neighborhood, my community, my city, I wanted to be helpful," recalls Stern. "I simply rearranged my practice so I could do this, and that felt right to me."

COURTESY OF MICHELE TURK

I was listening to the radio in my kitchen, and heard that something had happened to the World Trade Center. I went out on my front doorstep and I could see smoke coming up. I could hear sirens. I stood there for a while wondering what could be happening, then I heard the second airplane. Manhattan is very narrow downtown, and the second plane was very low, so it was noticeably louder than any airplane should have been—it was startling.

One airplane had crashed into the World Trade Center, and then to hear another one, you began to understand that it wasn't an accident. There was an ominous feeling—you just knew something terrible was happening. I felt stunned and I thought, *"What should I do?"*

Then I realized that I'm a Red Cross volunteer—I can *do* something. It was an immediate connection—surely I can be helpful somehow because I had the venue through which I could do something useful. I'd taken the courses only weeks earlier.

Before the towers fell, I left my house and made my way up to the Red Cross on Amsterdam Avenue. It was bedlam up there. There were hundreds—multiple hundreds—of people who had converged on the Red Cross. People just flowed into the building. That first day it was the kind of chaos one finds at a terrible event. New Yorkers wanted to do something. Everybody was feeling the need to do something, because doing something relieves one's own anxiety.

I stayed for about eleven hours that first day, but I was not sent out. I kept thinking I had something important to give, but I spent the day waiting around for someone to tell me where I should go.

I went home about eleven at night and I came back early the next morning, around seven. Things were beginning to take shape by then.

I spent the day in an auditorium at New York University Hospital at 30th Street and First Avenue, where the morgue is. Family members were coming to register missing persons with the police department. There was a very long, long line going up First Avenue—it was many, many blocks. Fortunately it was warm and sunny—it was beautiful weather in those days.

I was there as an emotional support person, mostly outside talking to people waiting in line. When you're working a disaster—this ongoing traumatic experience—you're not talking to people who have made a decision to delve into the psychological issues in their lives, who make an appointment and come to your office. You're talking to people who are caught in the net of this frightening and destructive experience, and they need to find their way through it.

Later that day we were moved to another building, part of Bellevue Hospital several blocks downtown. The auditorium was smaller, and once again, not everyone could fit. It was quite warm and people were getting overheated. A desk was set up inside the front door where people could register their family member's name, then they were taken into the auditorium where they had to wait several hours before they were called to an interview with a detective.

At that point there was a lot of panic and fear and confusion, as well as a lot of buzz that people might be in shock and wandering around somewhere. There was still hope that people would be found. Posters with photos were going up all over the place. Families kept asking for lists of hospitals with patients to see if their relative's name was on them. People were desperate, some were crying. It was that mixture of things that people who have been affected by a trauma initially feel. You sort of feel everything—anxiety, worry, fear, anger. There was an enormous emotional cloud over everything.

When messages began to ripple back in line that the detectives were asking for hairbrushes and toothbrushes to get DNA samples, that sent panic through the room. It meant that people would have to say, "This is my son who is missing, and this is his toothbrush." Most of them hadn't gotten that far along in their reactions yet—that somebody is definitely dead, and they're going to have to identify the body, or the body won't be recognizable enough to identify.

As a mental health worker in a crisis, there's not much to *do*. You don't go elicit feelings, you don't ask probing questions. What you do is offer the families or friends the sense that they're not alone, that there are people who care, that people are taking care of the situation, and that they will get information as soon as it's available. For some, it's a handshake, or an arm on their shoulder, a kind word or look or a glass of water. None of it's rocket science—it's human contact and support.

It's good to be trained, but anybody trying to be useful, not intrusive, on the scene of a disaster is helpful. For the most part it's just being there—it's bearing witness to people's experiences. Everybody's a thera-pist when you're doing disaster work—people are going to feel better and feel comforted by your presence. That's what the Red Cross does.

People were grateful that the Red Cross was there. They know the Red Cross—everyone knows the Red Cross. It's an immediate response—you don't need to explain anything, or say, "I'm here to see if I can do anything to help you." They feel comfortable because you are Red Cross. It was definitely a reassuring symbol to them.

The next week I was at Pier 94 for a couple of shifts. Then I was sent on an ERV for three nights, from 6 P.M. to 6 A.M. We went down to Ground Zero, in front of P.S. 234, an elementary school. The Red Cross people I met were from all over—some of them had driven here from across the country. They hear about a big disaster, word goes out through Red Cross lines, and they jump in these trucks and barrel across the U.S. Most of these people had been in quite a few disasters together—they all knew each other and they come together at disasters.

I was the only mental health person in the ERV at that point, and this was the first disaster I had worked. Most of the other people had not had a mental health volunteer assigned to their truck at a disaster, and they made shrink jokes and crazy jokes. I thought, *"This is so embarrassing, they don't want me here".* Someone with my background was unfamiliar to them, and they weren't quite sure what the point of having me was in this situation. They saw utilizing counseling in any way as a weakness.

But a mental health volunteer can contribute a certain dynamic and understanding and a certain way of seeing what's going on with the people who need help. I didn't see myself doing big-deal counseling or saving people. I saw my role as helping them get through this awful time knowing that they're not all alone, and maybe showing them that they were not weak if they wanted to talk to somebody about how they were feeling.

Next, I was sent to the boat, the *Spirit Ship,* three days a week. On the ground floor there was food, two buffet lines and plenty of coffee. It was catered from local restaurants—the food was incredible. I'll never forget one day they served little salmon packets baked in phyllo pockets. Guys were coming in covered in dirt and mud and here they were eating salmon out of little pouches.

Upstairs on the ship there were a few places for people to sleep and they had massage therapists giving massages. There were also two decks where one could stand and hang out and look at the river. So when the people working on the pile—the big heap of rubble at Ground Zero—came in, they were really someplace else, away from the scene of the disaster.

We were circulating on the top and bottom decks and around the food tables, where we would sit and have a cup of coffee or a meal and talk to workers as they came aboard. They needed to talk, but much of the time, they didn't want to talk about their feelings. Instead they talked about what they were doing, how terrible this was, how hot it was, how hard the work was, how the soles of their shoes were worn, and how happy they were to be there, to be able to do something.

The first time someone spontaneously approached me, I was sitting on the *Spirit Ship* and a crane operator who had come in for lunch came up to me. He was from New Jersey, medium height and dark hair, in his thirties, and he was wearing a t-shirt and blue jeans. The tables were long, narrow, cafeteria tables and sitting across from each other we were quite close.

He was saying that operating a crane was the hardest work he had ever done. It was a sort of running conversation, slightly manicky—a constant stream of talking, just all over the place. Then he stopped and looked up at me, right in my eyes, which was unusual because those guys didn't tend to be that direct. His eyes didn't move from mine—it must have been thirty seconds.

"You know what happened today?" he said. His eyes filled with tears, but he didn't cry. "I found a leg from the knee down."

He didn't know how to process this. He was as surprised by what he said to me as I was—he didn't plan to talk about it, but he couldn't keep it in. He was stunned and shocked—like getting smacked. It scared him, it horrified him—he wanted to run from it. You could see that he was desperate to find a way to go back and do his work, and you could see he didn't know how he was going to go back.

"I imagine that was scary and startling," I said. "That must be very difficult for you to have had that experience."

We started talking about how the family of the person whose leg he found is probably wondering what happened, and now they would be able to know. We talked how this was a "gift" for family members because they could begin the healing process. Afterwards he felt more in control of himself and more able to go back to operating the crane. Everything wasn't all better, by any means, but talking about the incident enabled him to deal with it. As a mental health volunteer, my job is to cast a wide eye—not to intrude, but to see that people seem all right. There's a wide range of what's "all right" on a disaster because there are a lot of bizarre things happening. Calm people can become emotional, and emotional people can become absolutely silent.

Firefighters were particularly shut off at first—theirs is a very close, closed community. Before 9/11, they didn't go to therapists. They thought they didn't have any need for a mental health person—they laughed at that. When they were with the guys, they wouldn't talk because *guys don't do that.* But if you got one of them alone, he would want to talk.

A very touching experience happened just before Christmas. I was sitting down with one of the firefighters under the big white tent. He looked so tired, so beat.

"Can I have a cup of coffee with you?" I asked.

"Okay," he said.

"How you doing?" I asked. His face just dropped. "You know, I have three daughters—I missed all their birthdays. I missed my anniversary. I've missed everything," he said. "And I'm still here."

He was feeling terrible. He was desolate. He was walking around this grim scene every day, exhausted, for hours. And he'd get home and be too tired to do anything and couldn't think of anything else, so even when he wasn't there, he was still there in his mind.

This firefighter was so torn between his family and this mission— not this job but this *mission* which he *had* to do—he couldn't *not* do it. As we all know for firefighters, their fellow firefighters are sometimes more "family" than family. It's a very strong allegiance and a very powerful, intimate, important bond in their lives. In doing this job, he had missed his children's birthdays and his anniversary and he was horrified at himself.

We talked for forty-five minutes or so and I think he felt better afterwards. The next day, I was looking for him because I had gotten some stuffed animals from the Red Cross for him to take home to his daughters. But when he came in for lunch, he came up and tapped me on the shoulder. "I want to show you pictures of my family," he said.

Talking to me made him feel he had a connection with a human— that someone cared—and it was a way for him to reconnect to his family. He felt that he had been separated from his family, and missed out on all these family events that were important. His wife was probably furious with him, the kids were wondering where dad was, and he didn't know how to get back to his family. This was a beginning.

What stays with me from the whole experience is a real love of doing disaster work. I came away with a deep appreciation of the Red Cross for providing the agency through which I can do it. It's a forum for people like me to go out and do things that give our lives meaning, and hopefully, we can help other people at the same time. And that's pretty wonderful.

After the Red Cross stopped providing mental health services at Ground Zero, Virginia Stern continued as a volunteer one day a week with the September 11 Recovery Program assisting staff with mental health and administrative issues.

Stern now lives in Clinton Corners, New York and volunteers as a DAT member with the Dutchess County chapter of the Red Cross.

Linda Fink
Cincinnati, Ohio

Linda Fink is a social worker who began her Red Cross career at the Butler County chapter in Hamilton, Ohio, nearly thirty years ago. After four years, she moved to Cincinnati, where she is the director of response and labor services for the Cincinnati Area chapter of the American Red Cross. She is responsible for client service delivery programs, including disaster services, case work with military personnel and their families, and international services.

Fink spent a month in New York City after 9/11. As the family services officer, she supervised the work of several hundred volunteers and staff who met with families and provided them with various services and financial aid. It was among the most taxing jobs, physically and emotionally, in her nineteen years of disaster work.

I arrived in New York City about a month after 9/11. The Red Cross had already set up what we call "service delivery sites" where family services staff can sit down, one on one, with each family. We talk to them about how they were affected, what their immediate needs are, and how they're going to recover from the emotional, physical, and material losses that they incurred because of the disaster. We also try to help families determine what their own personal resources are, what the community resources are, and what Red Cross has available to assist them with their recovery. We make a very simple step plan that outlines how they are going to get through the next few hours, or the next day. Disasters find people in a variety of situations, so the plan we create depends on where the client is in the grieving process, and what their coping skills are.

By the time I arrived the tragedy had pretty much sunk in. There are different phases that an individual goes through when they suffer a loss of that magnitude. If it's a fatality of a family member, there's the shock and the disbelief, and then sometimes there's also anger. I think anger set in faster on this particular disaster because someone perpetrated this—it wasn't an act of God or something that could necessarily have been prevented.

Fear was probably the number one thing that we dealt with. New Yorkers aren't scared easily. They pride themselves on their resilience and ability to handle high-stress situations. So this was new to the people of New York—their way of life had been threatened. They were also worried about the possibility of future attacks.

The family assistance center at Pier 94 was set up to work with just those who had lost family members. It was a place where families could come together to grieve, and get whatever help they needed, whether it was from the Red Cross or another agency. There were hot meals available continually, childcare and toys for the children, a memorial wall with pictures and flowers and mental health workers who could spend time with grieving families.

When I arrived the service centers were in full swing. Yes, people had to stand in line, and they were angry at the processes involved in getting through the system. Whether you're in New York City or in Florida, lots of times there are more clients than workers. That's a constant struggle for the organization. We don't like clients standing in line, and clients don't like standing in line, but sometimes it's unavoidable in order to get that one-on-one relationship built between the caregiver and the client. As much as I don't like it, all we can do is assure the public that it's like when you go to the doctor's office, and there is a sign there that says: "Excuse us if you have to wait, but we will give you the same time and attention when it is your turn."

The Red Cross also set up an "800 number," where people could call from virtually anywhere in the country and reach a caseworker twenty-four hours a day to talk about their needs related to September 11th. This was a way to help people without having them come to one of our centers. We also did a lot of outreach—we would knock on doors in lower Manhattan and ask, "Do you have any needs related to September 11th?"

When someone called the hotline and needed help urgently—maybe they needed medicine replaced or they were house- or apartment-bound and couldn't or were afraid to go out—we sent a team of family service workers called "hotshots." Sometimes we would send a nurse or mental health worker with them. If you sent a team of ten workers to a high-rise building that had hundreds of apartments in it, it wasn't long before the word spread, and then you had lines forming outside the apartment building too. We tried to match our resources, particularly our human resources, to the needs, but it was rather difficult even though people sometimes worked around the clock.

And the families had some real concrete needs. Not only were they trying to get over the shock and grief of losing a family member, but oftentimes he or she was the breadwinner. I remember one lady who had some sort of physical illness—I think it was multiple sclerosis. Her husband was killed on 9/11. Before he died he had been remodeling the bathroom so that she could get in there with her wheelchair. And so not only is she a widow grieving for her husband, but she physically could not use the facility on her own. That was an urgent need, and we were able to send a contractor in there to get that done so that she was could remain in her apartment.

Then there were the ongoing problems of people who worried how they would pay their bills. Many people lost their jobs in that instant, and so even though the disaster didn't affect their home, or them physically, they had no way to make ends meet. So that became a challenge for us, because that is not something that we normally deal with. But in this instance, we provided financial assistance for those who lost their jobs, to help them keep those basic things going.

Our typical disaster client does not have insurance or many personal resources. Some of the people we were seeing after 9/11 were not what we would call typical disaster clients. Their kids went to private schools and they belonged to country clubs—they had been living a lifestyle, not above their means, but with some heavy debt. Many of the people who died worked on a bonus schedule, and at the end of the year they received hundreds of thousands of dollars in bonuses. Throughout the year, they accumulated debt, then at the end of the year they got a bonus that would wipe it out before the next year. The wife usually didn't work so a stay-at-home mom suddenly became saddled with all of this debt. Life insurance was not paying, as one might expect, because there was no death certificate.

These families were left with pretty much no resources and big debts. So we helped them financially to pay their bills, whether they were for school tuition or the car in the driveway. We might ask, is that really important? But for them it was. Red Cross assistance is not based on how much money we have, or what is coming in. We deliver service based on the need. Our job in family services is to interpret what the families' needs are, and that's what we did after 9/11. We would look at their bills and determine what was the most immediate need—rent, utilities, car payments and food. It was imperative that we sit down with these families, get to know them, understand how their family had been living, what the families themselves felt was important, and then create a recovery plan that would meet all of their needs—emotionally, financially and materially.

We did not necessarily have a rulebook to go by on this one. We needed to get money, significant money, into these peoples' hands. The Red Cross came up with a plan called the Family Gift Program, which was a program of significant initial financial assistance, and then subsequent gifts were given to families based on need. We had a massive check-writing operation in New York City.

We also dealt with the paycheck-to-paycheck people. Some unemployment assistance was available for people who had lost their jobs, but that takes a while to kick in, however, so we paid rent and security deposits when necessary while these people looked for other jobs. While they might not have lost anybody, and their homes weren't damaged, lots of them were not in a good financial situation to start with, and they didn't have insurance to rely on.

One of the most common needs we encountered was relocation. People who were living in apartments where the glass had been blown out, or the air systems had to be shut down because of dust, had to move out. Finding an apartment in New York City is not an easy thing. Most of the time New Yorkers use a real estate broker. The Red Cross helped not only in terms of very high rent and security deposits, but we also had to pay broker fees because people just didn't have the money to do that.

By the time I left in mid-November, we had seen a good many of the families, and I think the lines reduced while I was there. When I got there a month earlier we had about twenty-five thousand cases, and by the time I left we had over thirty-six thousand. We had gone through the first round of getting about three months worth of assistance to families. They were entering another phase of the operation, which was making a plan to get additional money into the families' hands.

Hearing these kinds of stories over and over is taxing on a person's emotions. Plus, we put in very long days. And that's okay—people don't mind doing that, but the need continued for weeks and months and that was difficult. Besides, helping people grieve is not an easy task. Some workers could not get over some of the losses and the families' experiences. Once I leave a disaster relief operation I work at putting those in the back of my mind, because it's too painful to dwell on them. Otherwise, I probably would not be in this business any longer.

While I was in New York, I worked every day for thirty days. Nobody can work from 7:00 A.M. to midnight for a month without getting exhausted, and I was, emotionally and physically. When I got back home, it took me about ninety days to recover. Coming from tragedy like that back into normal life—job, family, home—*what an adjustment.* There was a lot of guilt on my part because I felt I was not able to make as much change as I would have liked in a month's time. The job was so huge. I knew it would take months to complete. Disaster workers are used to going in and helping people and helping the local chapter get over the hump, but this was a mountain that we had to climb.

Linda Fink spent a month in Florida after Hurricanes Charley and Frances in 2004 and was on assignment for three weeks after Hurricane Katrina in 2005.

James G. Cusic III
Fairview Heights, Illinois

*A*s a child growing up in Baltimore, Maryland, James "Jim" Cusic spent summers visiting relatives on the Eastern shore. One day Cusic's eight-year-old brother, Eamon, tripped on a loose board on a pier and fell in the water. Cusic, who was nine at the time, had just learned to swim and knew better than to attempt a rescue, so he could only watch helplessly as his brother bobbed up and down in the water. Fortunately the boy's uncle jumped in and rescued the child.

The incident left a lasting impression on young Cusic, who decided then and there that he "wanted to do something in the lifesaving realm." He started taking first-aid classes in the Boy Scouts and lifesaving classes from the Red Cross. As a teenager in Clinton, Connecticut, he became a water safety instructor at seventeen, the minimum age, and took advanced first aid as well.

While he was attending the University of Maryland at Baltimore County, a friend suggested that he look into joining the air force as a pararescueman—a paramedic who specializes in search and rescue using skills such as parachuting, scuba diving and mountain climbing. (Pararescue teams were among the military units used that rescued residents of New Orleans stranded on

COURTESY OF JAMES CUSIC
James Cusic

*rooftops by Hurricane Katrina.) He enlisted in the air force in March 1980
and was accepted into a pararescue training team.*

*Cusic spent the next twenty-two years in the air force in various locales
on assignments, eventually rising to the rank of major. He says he used
his lifesaving skills many times, both on the job and off. In the summer of
2001, Cusic was stationed at the Pentagon in the Special Operations section working for the chairman of the Joint Chiefs of Staff—a central point
for updates from special operations from the field. It was his last assignment
before he was slated to retire.*

O n the morning of September 11th, I was on the first floor of
the Pentagon in a medical clinic getting my neck worked on.
We were watching the replays on TV of the first airplane hitting the
World Trade Center. When we saw the second one hit live we all knew
something was wrong and I immediately returned to my office.

When our building was hit by American Airlines Flight 77, we were
still watching TV. The newscaster said the Pentagon was on fire. I remember thinking, *"This is not happening."* Working in the Pentagon,
you're prepared for military actions overseas. But to have it happen not
only on our own soil, but in my place of employment—that was surreal.

All the big bosses went to a staff meeting in the National Military
Command Center (NMCC)—it's the hub, so to speak. They sent
runners to our office to keep us updated. One of them told us where
the building was hit—almost exactly on the other side of the building
from where we were located. Because the Pentagon is made of very
thick timber and lots of concrete, and I work in a skiff—a room with
thick walls and no windows—I didn't feel it and I didn't hear it either.

The Pentagon has five rings, or five hallways, going left to right,
and five stories, plus a couple levels underground. There was only one
ventilation system for the whole building. Black soot and smoke was
coming out of the vents. My first inclination was to leave. We stayed in
case we were needed and we used plastic bags and duct tape to seal the
ventilation outlets in our own offices. But after about fifteen minutes,
we made the decision to leave because we were not needed right there
and it was getting hard to breathe. We also thought a second plane

might crash into the building.

As I left the building I ran straight into the triage area where they were already taking care of people. My medical training took over and I started going to work. We treated sixty-five people in the north parking lot of the Pentagon and saw that they were transported safely elsewhere. We used ambulances, we used government cars—anything we could—to get them out. Because the building was under construction, there were some loose boards lying around, and so we used them as stretchers and carried people out. We also had these little golf carts—the Pentagon was actually built so the generals could drive their vehicles all the way into the building and up to their offices. Later, somebody figured out it wasn't a good idea with all the exhaust, but they still have golf cars that the maintenance folks use, and that's what we were using to evacuate the wounded.

After they were all taken care of a man with a megaphone called out for volunteers to go back into the building and search for more survivors. Of course, I volunteered, and because I'm a medic, I was at the front of the line. We put a t-shirt or rag over our faces to prevent smoke inhalation. We entered the building and stopped in the restrooms and wet the t-shirts, and then made our way to the center courtyard.

When we—Rick Arnold, also a Scout leader—and several other co-workers got to the interior, we couldn't see where the plane hit the building, but we could see smoke. There were actually pieces of the airplane on the inside of the courtyard. At that point, there was only one fire truck in there. Because the building was built so many years ago, some of the newer fire engines couldn't get inside the courtyard because the passageway was not high enough for them.

When we tried to go towards the fire, the firemen stopped us—they were coming back out because the smoke was too intense. That's when we set up the triage area in the Pentagon courtyard. We had four different categories: "immediate needs," those with life-threatening injuries; "walking wounded," injured but okay; "delayed," the ones that have injuries that are not life-threatening but need care, such as abdominal injuries or burns that weren't critical; and "pending"—those that were probably going to perish. I told Lt. General Paul Carlton—

the Air Force Surgeon General—who was in charge, that I was a PJ. That's the nickname for "pararescue," the term for a person trained to do medical rescues in combat. He assigned me to the "immediate" category.

We continued to try to reenter the building, but were turned away again as we had no protective clothing. More medical personnel arrived, and we regrouped to reevaluate our position. It turned out that the person in charge of the "walking wounded" was no longer with our group, so I took over that group.

I also decided that this group would include the firemen and women, not just the people injured in the building. It was ninety-two degrees that day, with at least that much humidity, there was little breeze, and the firefighters had heavy protective clothing on. They would inevitably become dehydrated. One of the firemen had gotten so dehydrated he passed out so we gave him an IV and sent him to the hospital. Someone in the group opened a vending machine,

COURTESY OF THE AMERICAN RED CROSS

James Cusic, second from right pictured with volunteer Peter Macias, Scott Conner, vice president of health and safety and former Red Cross President Marty Evans

and we emptied the soda cans and filled them with water so that when the firemen came out, we could dump cans of water on their heads and down their backs. While we were doing this, the incident commander on the inside who had radio contact told us that the Twin Towers had gone down and a plane also had crashed in Pennsylvania.

The one person I remember the most is a gentleman with a scalp laceration. I talked to him initially to see what kind of mental state he was in. He was talking to me, and he seemed fine. I asked him, "What hurts?" And he said, "My head hurts." I asked him if he was cold, and he said no, but he was visibly shaking, and his color was kind of pale, which indicated he was going into shock. At that point, we got him an

IV and wrapped him up. He was put on top of the list for evacuation.

I stayed there until about 7 P.M., when it was obvious that no more survivors would be found. The next day, I was part of a team working in the NMCC to make sure we had the air fighters up to protect our airspace. If you remember at that time, all other aircraft were grounded. We were still trying to locate everybody who had been in the building the day before to make sure we had accounted for them. We got updates on the deceased.

Looking back, I don't think I did anything out of the ordinary— this is what I trained to do. Yes, I saved lives. Did I put myself in danger? Sure. But a lot of people did that day. Even today, if I'm in the backyard and I hear two cars crash, I grab the cell phone and the first-aid kit, go to the corner and start doing what I've got to do.

In October 2002, Major James G. Cusic III was awarded the American Red Cross Certificate of Merit in a ceremony at national headquarters in Washington. The award is given to staff or volunteers who have saved a life using the skills and knowledge learned in a Red Cross health-and-safety course. He was the only person to receive this award from the American Red Cross for the September 11th relief operation. Cusic also received an Air Force Commendation Medal, and the Boy Scouts' highest award, the Honor Medal with Crossed Palms.

Cusic retired from the military in October 2002. His first civilian job was as a disaster specialist for the St. Louis Area chapter of the Red Cross, where he managed the seventy-five-person disaster team and presented programs to the community to prepare for emergencies, such as the "Together, We Prepare" initiative launched after 9/11.

In 2003 Cusic became a counter-terrorism analyst at Scott Air Force Base in Illinois. He lives nearby with his wife and four children. In his spare time, he continues to teach Red Cross CPR and water-safety courses and volunteers with the disaster team across the river at the St. Louis, Missouri, chapter. He also teaches first-aid and water-safety classes to local Boy Scout troops.

Vicki North
Sweet Home, Oregon

The Baton Rouge River Center on the banks of the Mississippi has played host to everything from the Ringling Brothers Barnum & Bailey Circus to the Moscow Ballet. But after Hurricane Katrina, the ten-thousand-seat arena was transformed into the largest shelter for hurricane victims in the state. Two arenas were lined with cots and in some cases, residents cordoned off areas with a heap of hoarded clothes, paper products and other necessities distributed at the shelter. Vicki North, a therapist who volunteers with the Oregon Pacific chapter, arrived at River Center three days after the hurricane—just as rising flood waters forced the evacuation of thousands of New Orleans residents into Red Cross shelters along the Gulf Coast and elsewhere.

After the shooting at Thurston High School in Springfield, Oregon, in 1998, there was widespread concern in the local mental health community that there was no plan for mental health professionals to mobilize in a community-wide disaster. A group of us contacted the local Red Cross and learned that they have been training mental health people to do disaster work for years. About twenty of us decided to get the training in February of 2000, and then I joined the national disaster response team.

COURTESY OF MICHELE TURK
**Vicki North at
River Center shelter**

In July, just after hurricane season started that year, I was sent to my first disaster, Hurricane Allison in Texas. Going felt bold and different, so different from the way I use my skills in my private practice, where I see patients with mood, personality and eating disorders, and deal with trauma and abuse. I was hooked immediately.

What was most compelling for me was to be among the other Red Cross workers. Every one of them was making a tremendous sacrifice—they left their families and their ordinary lives for two to three weeks at a time and focused on helping the victims of destruction. To see myself as someone of that caliber was pretty heady stuff, and I liked identifying myself that way—as a Red Cross volunteer.

I try to do at least one disaster every year. It's challenging for me because when I don't work and see my regular clients, I don't get paid. My next disaster assignment was a local windstorm in my hometown. And after 9/11 I was in the New York area twice—I arrived three days after 9/11 and went back again in early November. I stayed about two weeks each time. I worked a flood in San Antonio the next summer and the next year I was in Maryland and Delaware for Hurricane Isabel. I was in Florida again in 2004 for Hurricanes Charley and Frances.

This year my assignment was Katrina. I flew into Houston and drove to Baton Rouge. I arrived early Thursday morning, September 1, three days after Katrina made landfall. The next day I was assigned to work in River Center shelter. There were almost seven thousand people in the shelter when I first arrived. I have never been in a group of that many people. Actually, that's the population of the town where I live, Sweet Home. We are spread out over a large geographical area, so this was really unlike anything I was used to.

When I do shelter work, the challenge is to meet and greet and see to the needs of every person in the shelter. Granted, one person can't meet everyone, but we worked as a team, and we went through the crowds and spoke with everyone we could make eye contact with, or whom we felt we could approach. If someone was sleeping we didn't interrupt them. We assessed the emotional and physical needs of as many people as we could in the shelter every day. We were also responsible for tending to the stress level of the other Red Cross workers. It's very emotional working with people in such distress, and sometimes the volunteers need to talk to someone about what they are experiencing themselves. We were fortunate, however, as our shelter was pretty well staffed with mental health workers. Counting local volunteers, we had anywhere between eight and sixteen staff during the day working the crowd, and four on the night shift.

When I first got there, people were dealing with shock, denial, disbelief and grief. That this was the reality—it was hard to believe. Most people definitely needed someone to talk to and someone to create a plan and assist them in carrying it out.

I slept in the ballroom of the Marriott Hotel in Houston the first night I arrived, and the next two nights I stayed at a Baton Rouge staff shelter in a church near River Center. Then one of the local volunteers offered his home, so another volunteer and I stayed with him and his wife for a few days. Next, a local doctor offered his lake house, about a forty-minute drive from Baton Rouge, and so six or seven of us stayed there. After working for twelve hours, getting away from the shelter to a somewhat peaceful place helped a lot. We were living with people we didn't know very well, but at least we weren't living with a hundred and fifty people we didn't know well, like at the staff shelter.

At River Center, we had two fully staffed twenty-four hour a day medical clinics, which were busy. There were many diabetics who came without medicine, people on psychotropic medications such as anti-depressants, and the normal medical problems of a group of people that large—a lot of the residents came down with illnesses and some had chronic illnesses or wounds that needed to be dressed. We even had a case of cholera. We got them the meds they needed as quickly as we could, and those with severe mental health issues were sent to other facilities as soon as possible.

Snacks were offered at certain times of the day, and volunteers from the local community passed out toys. There was even a school that opened in the shelter in a nice open area overlooking the Mississippi River. Each of the two shelters inside River Center also had a donated TV and there was another TV for kids to play video games.

Living in a shelter is better than being out in the elements, but it's a tough situation to be in. Physically it was challenging to be among that huge number of people—even for myself. This was the first disaster I had nightmares about after I came home. Part of the stress for the residents was the constantly changing population, so the people you came to the center with, and who became your neighbors—the people you bonded with—left and someone new took their place. In this kind of situation, people bond immediately, and when they are split up, that's a new loss to process. Many of those who didn't function well in the shelter environment were moved to other facilities that could care for them. But sometimes just moving them to another part of the shelter—one part was dim compared to other parts that were bright and noisy—often helped.

Most of the shelter residents came from New Orleans. We didn't get many who had been in unsafe places or had terrible deprivation like those who went to the Superdome or the Convention Center. Those weren't Red Cross shelters, by the way—but simply places to go to get out of the rain—and they were abysmally managed. So the people at the shelter where I was were traumatized by the storm itself, but not by its aftermath.

Some didn't know where loved ones were, and their anxiety level was high. I showed up for work one morning and one of the nurses came in and said, we have a lost boy and we need someone to help him. His name is Joshua and he's fourteen. He left his mother at home and went to the Superdome on his own just before the storm hit land. He had been listening to the news, so he knew how bad it would be, and he tried to convince his mother to leave, but she wouldn't. He expected her to show up at the Superdome but she never did. After a couple of days he got really worried so he approached a sheriff's deputy. They had begun evacuating people from the Superdome by then and the sheriff's deputy thought Joshua's mother might be in Houston at the Astrodome, so he took Joshua there. Joshua looked there but he was unable to locate his family, so the sheriff's deputy brought him all the way to back to Baton Rouge to River Center. They put him to bed and the next day I entered the scene.

I walked him through the shelter first to see if he recognized anyone, then I took him over to a bank of phones. First he called home. There was no answer. He had called home when he was in Texas and no one answered. Then he called his mom's boyfriend's home and no one answered. He said he knew his mother's cell phone number, so I dialed and she answered the phone! She was in Illinois—I'm not quite sure how she got there. His little face just lit up like a firecracker when she answered the phone, and he was just as excited to find out his little brother was okay. We were able to arrange for a flight for him.* Two days later he flew to Chicago and joined his mom and his brother.

There were so many hurricane survivors like Joshua that were helped by Red Cross workers. So many . . . .

By the time I left after two weeks, most people had made some sort of plan for themselves, and the shelter population had diminished significantly to eighteen hundred. Those left had very little resources to begin with—they were people who were homeless or on public assistance or living marginally before the hurricane. Those are always the ones most profoundly impacted over the long haul.

River Center Shelter closed in October, 2005.

---

*Angel Flight America, which provides free air transportation for people in need of medical care, flew more than one thousand missions after Katrina to help relocate and reunite hurricane survivors.

Paige Roberts
Gautier, Mississippi

Paige Roberts grew up in Indiana and moved to Jackson, Mississippi in 1993 at age twenty-three, when she landed a job as a TV news reporter at WLOX, the local ABC affiliate. Two years later she married a local judge. Well steeped in the community, she worked in public relations for the Moss Point School district and taught broadcast journalism at Pascagoula High School before she began her current job as executive of the Southeastern Mississippi chapter of the American Red Cross in 2004.

Her only prior experience with the Red Cross was as a blood donor. Yet within a year, she faced six major storms, including Hurricane Ivan, which skimmed coastal Mississippi and came ashore in neighboring Alabama only five weeks after her first day on the job. Every time Roberts and her staff prepared for a major hit—making sure supplies were available, readying staff and partnering with local industry to lend a helping hand—they were spared the worst of the storms' fury. But these disasters were practice for what would come a year later, when Hurricane Katrina devastated Mississippi's coastline.

COURTESY OF GENE DAILEY

Three days before Katrina hit—Friday, the 26th of August—we started the day and didn't think much of it. It looked like Katrina would hit the bottom tip of Florida or Panama City on the panhandle. Then suddenly around 3:30 P.M., the whole forecast changed. And everyone—local emergency management, local industry leaders, the Red Cross—went into this frenzy because all of a sudden Katrina moved to the west and was headed right for us. Plus, there had been a noticeable change in the severity of the storm and urgency of our situation. But it still did not register in my mind what was about to occur.

Everything happened so fast—and whatever had to be done had to be done right then. But a lot of people who usually don't leave during a storm, such as our local volunteers, got skittish and left, which brought us down in manpower. We had so little time and such a small number of people doing it all—it was crazy. We secured the keys to the shelters, we ordered as much food as possible and we did a lot of shopping, pulling everything we needed—water, diapers, ice—off the shelves at the grocery store. We did staff schedules for shelters, then we distributed shelter kits to each of the ten shelters at local schools in Jackson and George counties.

We're an industrial-based county and we had local partnerships in place with Northrop Grumman Ship Systems, the biggest employer in the state. They provided two vans and two drivers to help us distribute goods to the shelters. They had just finished building the U.S.S. *San Antonio*, so a crew of U.S. Navy sailors were around to help us load the vans and then unload them at the shelters.

On Sunday I got a call from the state civil defense director at 7 A.M. and he said, "You have to be here." I got dressed, grabbed a peanut butter and jelly sandwich and left. My husband, Gary, took our four-year-old son, Winston, and our seven-month-old son, Quincy, along with my mother and stepmother, to a motel at the intersection of Routes 63 and 10, which is about ten miles from the gulf.

Then I went to the emergency operations center (EOC) in downtown Pascagoula, which is in a building that houses the county supervisor's office. It's a solid concrete structure where we've always ridden out the storms. It's always the same people—firefighters, city representatives—so we all know each other. We work together throughout the year and we ride out the storms together. I stayed there overnight.

We opened the shelters around 4 P.M. on Sunday, August 29. We knew that when we opened the shelters it would be for about two nights—that's the most anyone here had heard of happening before. It had been raining and windy during the night, and we actually had to evacuate the EOC the next morning ourselves because some of the roof starting coming off. It wasn't until we evacuated—we went across the street to the courthouse—that we saw how bad the damage was. When we came out the cars parked outside of the building were completely submerged. The water was knee deep. It's one thing to watch the hurricane through the window and another to be in the middle of it.

There was a mandatory evacuation south of Route 9, and a voluntary—but strongly encouraged—evacuation south of I-10. The night before, we had parked our ERVs at the interchange of Routes 63 and 10. We had seven of them and six were flooded and ruined. In the entire county, more than 13,000 homes were destroyed. Thousands of others also sustained major damage, which means they are habitable but severely damaged. We had eleven fatalities here in Jackson County, but the neighboring counties were hit worse—eighty fatalities in Harrison, and fifty in Hancock.

On Monday I went to Pascagoula High School, the high school where I used to teach, and opened a shelter there. It wasn't planned but people being rescued in that area had no place to go. There was no one to staff it except Jay Huffstatler, a board member, and me. I had done a lot of planning for the shelters but I had never manned one—and certainly not for the night. It was less than ideal conditions—we didn't have running water—but it was someplace to get people inside to safety. We housed about eighty-five to one hundred people that night, including two babies that were four days old.

The first night I asked one of the young mothers of those babies if she was nursing. She said no, so I asked if she wanted to start. She said she had formula. Two days later, when I was back at the shelter, I asked her if her milk dried up, and she said no. I said, "The stores may not be open in two days to buy more formula and your baby will die if you don't start nursing." She said I could teach her in the back room. It just took some time but we were successful.

Meanwhile, I went to see what happened to my house on Tuesday. Our home was right on the gulf in Gautier (pronounced GO-chay).

I knew it was gone as soon as I heard that Beach Boulevard—an east-west boulevard that runs for about three miles along the shore in the next town, Pascagoula—didn't have a house standing on it. Even though it was made of brick, I knew that our house was obliterated.

When I got there I couldn't get my bearings. The entire foundation didn't even make it and there's a giant crater in the back where the pool was. I was wearing my wedding ring and before I left the house, I put the diamond earrings on that my husband bought me. Everything else was gone. There's a huge pile of debris in the front yard and what looks to be the frame of the house. Someone found my wedding dress in a tree. I found one unbroken piece of my everyday dishes and one piece of my fine china. There wasn't a lot to salvage or dig through—I found that a blessing because people who have flooded houses seem to have a harder time because their stuff is still there.

A neighbor who was crazy enough to stay during the hurricane watched the houses on the beach fall apart. He said our roof blew off first and with continual rain and the pounding of the surge, the whole house fell apart later. After Hurricane Georges, our house was totally fine. We also survived fine during Ivan. Katrina, on the other hand, was out worst nightmare as homeowners

COURTESY OF GENE DAILEY

Paige Roberts and a fellow Red Cross staff member surveying what's left of her home on the Gulf Coast

on the Gulf. She was relentless in her wrath—not a two-by-four or a brick was left in place. She even destroyed the trees we had planted to mark the births of each of our sons.

After we evacuated the EOC on Monday morning I had asked a police officer if there had been any fatalities. He said there was a baby floating in the water and nobody could get to her. I decided that whatever my personal losses were, they would pale in comparison to a woman who had lost her baby. Losing a house and all your possessions is a significant loss, of course, but it is nothing compared to what those who have lost loved ones are going through.

At this point I'm so focused on what I'm doing in my job that I can't fathom what will define normal for our family. We actually received financial assistance from the Red Cross. It was based solely on the number of people in the family and anyone in the affected disaster area was eligible. Our family qualified for $1,265. The storm hit two days before payday. It was the only thing I could do to help my own family because in every other way I was unable.

The toughest part has been being separated from my sons. The most time I had spent away from my kids were three days for Red Cross business trips. The health concerns early on were so grave that I didn't think being here was safe for an infant. I saw my family on Tuesday the 30th of August, then they went to Columbus, Georgia, where my husband's sister lives. Then they drove to Texas where my mom's family lives. I didn't see my sons for more than three weeks. My husband and my sons came back to Mississippi and stayed in Gulfport at my husband's parents' house for a couple of weeks. They are back in Gautier now with my mom, and I am staying at a hotel in Pascagoula.

In the first few days after Katrina made landfall it was surreal. Every time I thought to myself, *"This is so unbelievable,"* the next thing that happened was even more absurd. Nothing amazes me anymore. The week after the storm hit, I was attending meetings with mayors at one in the morning. One night I got ninety minutes of sleep.

In the beginning, many times I would go to visit people in their homes or on their property. The living conditions they were insisting on staying in were deplorable. It was just one family after another refusing to leave. Six weeks after the storm, people were still living in tents and children were running around barefoot in bayous with mosquitoes everywhere. One woman who lived in a trailer that was destroyed still has a wooden porch. She just sat there. I told her we have a shelter not far away. She said, "Thanks, honey, but no." When I told her a building or health inspector will come and condemn this place, she said, "That's when I'll leave."

Just last week I went to a mental health meeting. It's just so depressing. I hear of family situations where couples decided to separate since the storm—it's very difficult to be married right now. In addition, the drug and alcohol abuse and domestic abuse rates have increased already.

Everything has become so relative. What happened in New Orleans seemed to negate our devastation here in Mississippi. Yet the need I see is so overwhelming, and the response—both human and physical—so inadequate, that it's been frustrating. The resources that are available are less than satisfactory, to put it mildly.

It's been nearly two months, and we still have mobile feeding units in hard-hit neighborhoods, we're still doing bulk distribution of cleanup kits, comfort kits and some baby supplies, and providing mental health services and financial assistance. And we're still sheltering people. It's less hectic but not any less demanding than it was right after the storm. The challenges are different now.

My role is working closely with the fleet of out-of-town volunteers, and interfacing between the community my chapter serves and national headquarters. I've also been assisting with public affairs. Every morning I do a live radio interview. One of the challenges is communicating with the city, county and community leaders about what we're doing and why. I have to walk a fine line between corporate and community loyalty. I respect the organization and I understand why some decisions are made, but in the end I'm the one left here living with the people in the community. And I'm gonna make sure we're okay when it's all over.

One of the unpopular decisions was a change in Red Cross policy regarding who was qualified to receive financial assistance. At first, if you had some type of proof of residence, such as driver's license, or if you lived in a certain zip code, you received a set amount of money regardless of anything else. But after six weeks, the policy was changed so that now you have to have major damage, or a completely destroyed home, to qualify. This had to be done because the potential for fraud is so high, but also because so many people had already received aid. We have given away $120 million to people in a five-county coastal area in southern Mississippi.

We got into a sticky situation with national headquarters and the local NAACP. First, a few African-American politicians weren't happy with the lack of shelters and centers in their areas where people could get financial assistance. Then the local NAACP got involved, as did Red Cross national headquarters. The upshot was that we had to move a center two miles, even though it had been located in Moss Point, a predominantly African-American community, and there had been a lot of support for keeping it right where it was. The problem wasn't so much about racial politics, but about the fact that national headquarters and local Red Cross chapters are not always a good mix after a disaster. National headquarters didn't take into consideration that a community is more than demographics—it's about local dynamics and they didn't trust the judgment of the people who live and work here.

Then I got grief from several community leaders, including the mayor of Moss Point, who was concerned because the only two financial assistance centers in the county, were on the east side of the county—which is largely African American—and now we looked guilty of reverse discrimination. Now I was a racist. It never once occurred to me what color anyone's skin was. If they needed food, we were going to feed them, if they needed shelter, we were going to shelter them. It didn't matter to me if you were black, white, yellow or red.

Fortunately, the good I have accomplished has outweighed those incidents, and I am focusing on trying to get my chapter up and running again. Things are so up in the air. Our building got flooded so we are securing temporary office space. We're getting closer every day to being a better organization here, but it's still two steps forward, one step back. The most pressing challenge is that our revenues have been seriously cut back.

I've been in contact with local corporations about making up for lost revenue—funds we need to run the local chapter—but almost all of the money coming into the Red Cross is going to the general Katrina fund—not to the local chapter to help with day-to-day operations. Consequently, we can't do the kinds of things our chapter used to do pre-Katrina, and people in the community don't necessarily understand that. Besides myself, the chapter only has one other full-time, and two part-time employees. We were about to beef up our health and safety program and begin babysitting training, but that's not possible now. We will still be able to help single-family disaster victims because we have to, but beyond that absolute-must service I don't know what we're going to be able to provide for some time to come.

Paige Roberts and her husband have decided to rebuild their home in Gautier.

Part III

LIFELINES

Chapter 5

HOMETOWN HEROES

Life's most urgent question is what are you doing for others?
—Martin Luther King, Jr.

In the early 1900s Wilbert E. Longfellow, a young journalist from Rhode Island who covered the waterfront beat for a Providence newspaper, launched a one-man crusade to "waterproof America" and reduce deaths from drowning. Before long, he teamed up with the American Red Cross, and together, they launched the National Red Cross Lifesaving Corps in 1914.

Longfellow's campaign to teach all Americans to swim paid off. The Red Cross water-safety program became the gold standard of swimming instruction, and water sports also became safer. Longfellow's crusade coincided with a precipitous drop in the nation's drowning rate from about 9,000 deaths per year at the turn of the century to 4,000, where it stands today.

A century after Longfellow pioneered his water-safety campaign, American Red Cross health and safety programs that prepare Americans to save lives are so widespread that a majority of Americans learn to swim, or learn lifesaving skills, via Red Cross programs. Every year, nearly two million people sign up for Red Cross swimming courses, and 170,000 train for the Red Cross lifeguard exam.

The Red Cross trains another ten million people a year in other life-saving skills, from mainstays like CPR and first-aid classes to teaching people to use automated external defibrillators (AEDs), devices that analyze the heart's rhythm for abnormalities and deliver an electrical shock to restart the heart. Some chapters even teach CPR for pets.

"We either teach the courses, teach the people who teach the cours-es—first aid, CPR and lifesaving—or we support them," says Kathleen Pearson, director of health and safety for the Central New Jersey chap-ter. For example, a federal grant to make AEDs more widespread in ru-ral areas prompted the chapter to train 250 state troopers in CPR and the use of AEDs, and certified twenty of the state troopers as American Red Cross CPR/AED and first-aid instructors. Professionals such as EMTs, physicians and nurses, as well as organizations such as the Boy Scouts, Girl Scouts, 4-H and other civic groups, learn lifesaving and

COURTESY OF THE AMERICAN RED CROSS

**Commodore Wilbert Longfellow with members of the
YWCA Lifesaving Corps**

first-aid according to Red Cross protocol. The effects of the courses are far-reaching. Ordinary citizens gain the skills and confidence to enable them to give aid—and maybe even save a life—in an emergency. Every community in America has heartwarming stories of someone who became a hero simply because he or she put into action what was learned in a Red Cross course.

COURTESY OF THE AMERICAN RED CROSS

Bob Lenseth is a good example. Now CEO of the Westchester County chapter in New York, he began working for the Red Cross in 1968, and took many lifesaving courses over the years. In 1995 his seven-year-old daughter had a seizure and stopped breathing. Lenseth performed CPR and prevented possible brain damage.

In 2002 the local Red Cross taught employees of the Starbucks Coffee Roasting Plant in York, Pennsylvania, to use an AED. Eight months later fellow employee Arthur Conway suffered cardiac arrest on the job. Several of his fellow employees initiated CPR on him, and used the defibrillator until a pulse was detected.

Helen Despain of Kansas City, Kansas, took a lifesaving course when she was a nanny. Years later, a tornado tore apart the family's home and lifted her daughter off the sofa and pinned her beneath rubble. The girl stopped breathing. After she was pulled out, Despain remembered what she had learned in that long-ago course, and performed CPR until her daughter began breathing again.

While the people who actually save a life are heralded for their quick thinking and action, those who teach the courses usually go unrecognized. But not always. On her way home from teaching a CPR instructor's course a few years ago, Carleh Ward of Alexandria, Virginia, was approached by a young girl at the grocery store who tapped her on the shoulder. The thirteen-year-old asked her if she was Carleh Ward. When she said yes, the teenager said, "I just want to thank you. My mom who is over there took a CPR class from you last spring, and in December, my dad had a heart attack and she saved his life, thanks to things she learned from you."

Gaylord "Red" Colle
Ava, Missouri

*A*s a young boy growing up in rural Kansas, Gaylord "Red" Colle used to kick his feet playfully in a pond on the family farm, anticipating the day he would someday learn to swim. "From the time I was playing in that mud puddle in the pond, I always had it in my mind that I would swim," recalls Colle.

But it wasn't until Colle and his family moved to North Wichita when he was in junior high school, that he honed his swimming skills in a local watering hole. By the time Colle was in high school, swimming became his passion. In 1933, when he was a freshman, the swim coach at Wichita High School North asked Colle to try out for the swim team, and before long, Colle and his teammates won the state championship. During his junior year, Colle took a Red Cross senior lifesaving course and a water-safety instructor course. The next year he became a lifeguard at the municipal pool.

During World War II, he ended up in Washington and was one of the organizers of the water-safety, life-guard and first-aid courses taught there to government workers, under the guidance of Wilbert E. Longfellow. (By the time Colle met him, Longfellow had been given the title of "commodore" by the U.S. Volunteer Life Saving Corps for his work in bringing water safety to the masses). There were fewer than two hundred qualified first-aid instructors

COURTESY OF RED COLLE

when the war broke out and as a result of his efforts, there were nearly three thousand instructors by the war's end.

J ust before the war, in 1939, I got a temporary job with the Census Bureau in Washington, D.C. I was hired to help tabulate the 1940 census. My wife at the time, Billie, and I moved from Wichita, where we had run a municipal swimming pool. As Red Cross volunteers, we taught water-safety classes for the Sedgwick County Chapter. When I got to Washington, Billie and I went to the Red Cross to get our teaching authorizations transferred. The chapter director put me to work as a volunteer, teaching water-safety and first-aid courses at the indoor pool of the Ambassador Hotel. Billie got a job in the secretarial pool at Red Cross national headquarters.

I was about to get laid off from the Census Bureau because the job was done when a guy named Bob Duncan hired me as assistant director of First Aid, Water Safety, and Accident Prevention (FAWSAP) for the D.C. chapter of the Red Cross. I earned $140 a month. Although the draft was in effect, I had a deferment due to a bad knee.

At the time, Skipper Harold Enlows was the national director of the Red Cross safety program, and Commodore Wilbert Longfellow was director of water safety. I had already known Commodore because he had come to the Wichita chapter for a volunteer meeting and we held a dinner for him.

Skipper Enlows sent Commodore to us at the D.C. chapter to promote the first-aid program for emergency purposes. The war was on top of us and it was necessary for residents of Washington to get as much first-aid training as possible. The idea was that the United States might get bombed, and if it did, Washington would be a target.

Bob Duncan, another assistant director named John Gates and I met with Commodore for lunch in a restaurant in Georgetown. Together, we made a plan to put together as much first-aid training as we could for government workers.

There were three stages of the plan: First, we went with Commodore to all the directors of the various government agencies—Labor, Agriculture, the FBI, for example. Commodore would explain the program to them and why it was needed, and of course, it didn't need much selling—he was already so well known all over the East Coast.

The second stage involved teaching employees from each agency the basic training—standard first aid—followed by advanced and instructor training. In phase three, these people would teach standard first aid to other employees.

Many, many classes were taught during World War II. The program grew so fast—it was so popular. In 1942 we trained more volunteers than any year before. Back then only paid staff members were allowed to qualify as first-aid instructors, so Bob, John and I did most of the instructor training early on. But we expanded from three guys to five quickly, and field reps also came in from around the country to help teach instructors as fast as we could. We taught mostly government workers, but we also taught a lot of civilian classes. Night and day—we were going crazy—from morning to midnight.

I was assigned to the FBI. J. Edgar Hoover insisted that only paid staff teach the FBI because of security issues, but eventually they let us use some of the top volunteers. They were headquartered in the Justice Department at the time, but we taught down near Union Station. We taught mostly what was called "standard advanced first aid." It involves the three vital injuries: breathing, bleeding and poison. I taught thirty to forty agents a week, week by week by week, for about five years.

While I was in Washington, I also taught lifesaving at military bases where national headquarters used to hold its aquatic schools. We put on quite a few water-safety and swimming shows at Quantico Marine Corps base in Virginia, and other military bases, mostly to give the servicemen some entertainment. Commodore also staged shows at different places like the Takoma Park Pool in Maryland.

There were several versions of the program. For example, Commodore would set up a scene like a tropical island with palm trees and a beach, and he would teach the little ones to swim in the surf. Students dressed like mermaids of the South Pacific did synchronized swimming, and tumblers jumped off the diving board.

Commodore was known as a great showman. He was a big man, very outgoing, and he was known as the "amiable whale." He had all those sayings. There's a famous picture of him sitting on a rock dressed like King Neptune wearing a robe and a crown and holding a trident. Several of the sayings he was famous for were written in a fan behind him. They read: "Entertain them hugely while educating them gently!" and "Don't envy a good swimmer—be one!" and "Water is a good friend but a deadly enemy."

Of course, the aquatic schools did more than provide entertainment. They were designed to encourage similar programs in smaller cities and towns. But since you couldn't have a field rep traveling to every town, chapters sent instructors and volunteers to us wherever the schools were held.

For example, a town would hire some gal to be the head lifeguard to manage the pool. She may have had some swimming instruction, but she didn't know much about lifesaving. So we would get a scholarship for her and the little Red Cross chapter would send her to this training for ten days. She'd come back all sunburned with her clipboard, and she went home and taught other kids to be lifeguards.

The aquatic schools taught thousands of kids to be lifeguards into the 1970s or 1980s. Of course, Red Cross chapters all over the country still teach these classes to kids today.

Some of Red Colle's cousins recently told him they never thought he'd do anything with "that foolish swimming." But he made a career out of it.

Colle worked for the Red Cross for thirty-six years and continued as a volunteer for another twenty-five years. After he left Washington, D.C., in 1945, Colle served as director of First Aid, Water Safety, Small Craft and Accident Prevention Services for the Kansas City, Missouri chapter for the next twenty years. He later became manager of the Black Hills chapter in Rapid City, South Dakota, and in 1968, director of disaster services in Denver, Colorado. He retired in 1980. Colle continued as a Red Cross volunteer and received a fifty-year service pin in 1986. He remained a volunteer until 1995, when he moved to Ava, Missouri, where he resides.

Linda Jones, Maschel Rawlings & Lisa Roth
Mansfield, Texas

In the spring of 2003, a peanut butter and jelly sandwich got stuck in two-year-old Chase Patterson's throat. Chase's mother, Ginger Patterson, stuck her finger down the boy's throat. Fortunately, she was able to dislodge the sandwich—even though she didn't know the recommended procedure for choking victims.

Patterson was so shaken by the incident that she arranged for the local Red Cross chapter in Texas to teach an Infant and Child CPR class to fellow members of the Mansfield Moms Club . About ten women took the class, including Linda Jones and Maschel Rawlings, members of the Leapin' Lizards, a spin-off of the Mansfield Moms Club. "I took the class simply because everyone else was taking it and they say all moms should take the course," says Rawlings, who had taken a CPR course in high school years before. "I never thought I would use it." Not four months later, Rawlings performed CPR to save the life of Jones's son, Reilly.

While re-learning the proper technique was helpful, Rawlings says having the training so recently gave her the confidence to use the skills when she needed to. "Part of me was scared and afraid I wouldn't do the right thing," recalls Rawlings. "And the other part was saying, Just do something—even it isn't exactly by the book."

Jones, who shares her recollection of her son's rescue here, has since helped many others learn to be lifesavers.

Every week, the Leapin' Lizards, a group of about four or five women and their ten young children, meets for a playgroup at one of the members' homes. My friend Lisa Roth hosts the parties at her house because she has a pool.

It was Wednesday, July 23, 2003. After the kids had been swimming for a couple of hours, we decided to eat lunch.

When you walk out the door of the house there's a pool, then you go through a gate, and walk up a set of stairs onto a deck. There are tables set up in a big backyard with a play area. We fed the kids hot dogs, and then we started getting ready to go home. A pack of kids went back to the play area, and I thought Reilly, my three-year-old son, had gone with them.

I turned around to check on the kids and I could only see my older son, Griffin, who was five. You can't see the pool from where I was sitting on the deck, so I asked Maschel [Rawlings] if she saw Reilly anywhere, since Reilly had been sitting on the steps with her a few minutes earlier.

She stood up and screamed. Then she took off running. I was running right behind her. I immediately knew that Reilly must be in the pool.

COURTESY OF THE AMERICAN RED CROSS
Fire Chief Alex Rodriguez, Maschel Rawlings, Lisa Roth and Reilly and Linda Jones at a Red Cross ceremony honoring the lifesaving moms

He was floating face down in the deep end. Maschel jumped in and pulled Reilly to the side of the pool. Then I grabbed him and lifted him out of the pool. I thought that if I slapped him a few times he would be okay, but I could tell by his body weight that he was in trouble. He felt completely limp.

We laid Reilly down alongside the pool. His skin was blue. His eyes were open, but you couldn't see anything but the white part.

Maschel began CPR and Lisa called 911, then she ran back out to the pool. Maschel was kind of winded from pulling Reilly out of the pool, so Lisa took over doing CPR. She had been a flight attendant, so she had taken CPR training numerous times.

A little vomit was coming out of Reilly's mouth, but he really wasn't responding. It seemed like a really long time had passed, so I called 911 again. The lady who answered said, "You just called two minutes ago." It seemed like a half hour. At that point, I was hysterical. I was vomiting. I ran out front to flag down the ambulance.

When I got back, Reilly was breathing a little—but they were really shallow breaths. His skin was yellow but now you could see his eyeballs.

The ambulance, fire department and police all arrived at once. One of the first things the paramedics asked was whether Reilly was floating or if he sank. Since he was still floating when we found him, they knew he could only have been in the water one and a half to two minutes. Within thirty seconds, he probably went unconscious—little kids don't know how to hold their breath so he probably screamed and the water filled his lungs. The paramedics checked his vital signs and gave him oxygen. A normal person's oxygen levels are between ninety-five and one hundred. Reilly's was ninety-eight.

That was a good sign, but I was worried about brain damage, of course. We later learned that every minute you're not breathing you can lose ten to twenty percent of your brain functioning.

The "CareFlite"—a helicopter—landed on Lisa's front lawn and flew Reilly to Cook Children's Medical Center in Fort Worth, which is about twenty-five miles away. I left Griffin and Murphy, my one year old, at Lisa's house while Maschel drove me to Fort Worth. A chaplain met me at the hospital. My husband had also arrived.

Reilly was still unconscious and they were running tests on him, blood tests and a Cat-scan. The emergency room doctor said we wouldn't know anything for two or three hours.

Reilly and I were supposed to go to the Texas Rangers game that night. One of the first things he said when he awoke was "Are we going to the game?" We still hadn't gotten the results back on any of the tests, but the emergency room doctor said that was a good sign, and that he probably had minimal brain damage, if any. We stayed the night in the hospital because the doctors had to observe Reilly, but by the next morning, he was playing like nothing ever happened.

We are friends with some of the rescue workers who were the first responders, and we went to visit them the next day. The first thing David Gilmore, a fireman, said was, "You realize that if your friends hadn't done what they did, we would have had a different outcome?" I knew they had done a miraculous thing, but I don't think it hit home until then.

The next month, in August 2003, Mark James, director of health and safety for the Chisholm Trail Chapter, was scheduled to give a brief overview of CPR and first aid at the monthly meeting of the Mansfield Moms Club. He asked Linda Jones for permission to tell the story of how her friends helped saved Reilly from drowning. "I thought the other mothers would think I'm a horrible mom," recalls Jones. "Instead, it was the opposite—all of them said, 'Sign me up.'"

Since then, Jones has become an advocate for CPR training, and spreads the word every chance she gets. She and Maschel Rawlings have renewed their CPR training, and Jones has also signed up her husband, mother, and other members of her family.

In the first year after Reilly's accident, Jones, Rawlings and Roth were responsible for at least 150 people taking health and safety classes. The trio has also spoken at a number of Red Cross, community and church events, and has appeared on the local TV news several times.

In February 2004, Maschel Rawlings and Lisa Roth received the National Certificate of Merit Award, the Red Cross's highest lifesaving award for saving Reilly Jones from drowning.

A few months later, in May, Lisa Roth became a certified Red Cross CPR instructor and teaches classes to the local community. CPR training, says Roth "gives a person the confidence and almost permission" to act when someone needs help, noting that without formal training people sometimes are afraid to act, so they often don't do anything at all. "When you have that training behind you, your instincts kick in and you're on auto pilot— my body was almost moving without having to think," she says. "I hope the people I teach never have to perform CPR, but if they do they'll have the confidence to use it."

In the summer of 2004—one year after Reilly nearly drowned—he finally went swimming for the first time since the incident. At first, he refused to get in the water. But a skilled swim instructor helped him get over his fear. "They both went underwater and the instructor dunked Reilly," recalls Jones. "He came up from underwater and he was laughing and giggling." By the end of the summer, Reilly had learned to swim.

Kathleen Pearson
Brick, New Jersey

When Kathleen Pearson was six years old, her parents sent her to summer camp to learn how to swim. As a teenager, Pearson parlayed her passion for swimming into a summer job as a lifeguard. Eventually, her love of the water became the basis for a lifelong career as a Red Cross health and safety instructor and administrator. "I grew up with the Red Cross," says Pearson, Director of Health and Safety at the American Red Cross of Central New Jersey in Princeton. "And I have been involved in one way, shape or form for as long as I can remember."

At the age of fifteen, Pearson made her first save. Over the past twenty-five years, she has used her skills to save forty-eight lives. Although it seems like a lot of rescues for someone not employed as a paramedic, Pearson says that the rescues were simply the work of a Good Samaritan who took the time to help. "Some people joke and tell me that the two people they won't hang out with are Angela Lansbury and me because people are always dying around her and I'm always at the scene of accidents," says Pearson. "I ask them, 'How many accidents do you pass a week?' The difference is, I stop."

My parents were not the best swimmers, so they were concerned about their children since we lived in Hazlet, New Jersey, on the shore. So in 1971, when I was six years old, my parents shipped me off to a Girl Scouts camp about a half hour away in Farmingdale, New Jersey, to learn how to swim.

My first time going to class, I was shaking with fear. I met a woman named

COURTESY OF KATHLEEN PEARSON

Jean Bourne, the waterfront director and swim instructor. She started by trying to teach me to put water in my hand and put it on my face, but I didn't want to do it. When I tried to run away, I accidentally pushed her into the pool. I became her mission for the summer.

The second week of camp went a lot better. I would totally submerge my face in the water. By the end of the summer I was swimming. From that point on, whenever someone was trying to find me, they looked for me at the pool.

I went to the same camp for three to four weeks every summer until I was thirteen years old. Through the years, I went all the way up the ranks—beginner, advanced beginner, intermediate, swimmer, and I finally got my advanced swimmer certification.

At the age of fifteen, when it was time for me to get a summer job, I asked myself, What could I do around the water? Naturally I wanted to be a lifeguard. The camp I had attended offered a lifeguard course, and that's where I went. I stood there nervously with nine other lifeguard wannabes awaiting the arrival of our instructor. Who comes from around the corner but Jean. She just smiled at me—and I'm not sure if she was thinking, *Wow, I'm glad to see you in the class* or *Hmmmm, revenge.* Three weeks later I was a lifeguard.

Jean hired me on the spot, and so I was a lifeguard at the very pool where I had learned to swim. Two weeks later, one of the campers tried to go off the diving board, leapt too early, and hit her head on the end of the board. I waited a second to see if she would come up. When I saw blood, I knew I had to move. Jean, who was standing nearby, ran to the pool when she heard there was a problem. We both slid into the water. We put the girl on a back board while we were in the water in case she had a back injury, then we removed her from the pool. Once on deck, we treated the gash on her head, cared for shock by covering her and waited for the ambulance.

When it was all over, Jean and I cried in each other's arms. That's when I knew I was hooked. The feeling of being able to save someone's life and of knowing that your actions can make such a difference was incredible.

I went to the Red Cross to see how I could get more involved. For the next two years, I did everything from stuffing envelopes and making calls, to volunteering as a lifeguard for Red Cross swimming classes at a local pool. When I turned seventeen, I went on to get my Water Safety Instructor Certification so I could start teaching swimming and lifeguarding courses for the Red Cross. While I was a student at Kean College in Union, New Jersey, I worked as a lifeguard at the college pool and I continued to volunteer teaching swim lessons for the Red Cross.

The minute I graduated from college, I went to the Jersey Coast chapter, which was in Shrewsbury at the time, to complain that I hadn't received my swim-lessons cards certifying that I had taught certain classes. Someone said they'd pay me for a couple of months to come and help get them out quicker. I did and I never left.

Soon I was hired as an administrative assistant in the health and safety department. Meanwhile, I continued to take classes. Through the years, I became an instructor and then instructor trainer in every health and safety course the Red Cross offers—swimming, lifeguarding, first aid, CPR and then the highest level of lifesaving, called emergency response. In 1990 I also started taking disaster classes. I learned to teach all of the basic level Disaster Courses, and joined the DSHR.

I have never worked on a first-aid squad, but about half of the saves I made were while I was working as a lifeguard. The rest were just stopping at accidents.

One time I was walking down the boardwalk in Belmar, New Jersey, and I heard a man in the ocean yelling for help. It was 7 P.M. The lifeguards had already left.

He got caught in the rip tide. I swam out, grabbed the man and kept him floating until we were out of the current. Then I brought him ashore.

Another time, I was walking down the beach in Sea Girt, another Jersey shore town, and a man collapsed on the boardwalk. He had no pulse and he wasn't breathing, so I did CPR for about ten minutes until the ambulance got there.

A few years later, I was driving to Florida, and I saw a car accident in South Carolina. Two cars hit each other and one car flipped a couple times. The passengers had severe bleeding and broken bones so I administered first aid to try to stop the bleeding. I then had to treat two men, two women and four children for inline stabilization [keeping the victim's head, neck and back inline] so any movement would not cause further injuries.

A lot of the rescues have been while I was driving down the New Jersey Parkway and I stopped at an accident. It always surprises me that people drive by these things. There are a lot of reasons—fear of lawsuits, fear of diseases, fear of doing something wrong. They have to remember that doing something is better than doing nothing. Just stopping and calling 911 can save somebody's life.

My most recent save was on Christmas Eve morning in 2003. I was on my way to work at 6:45 A.M. when I came upon a car accident on a back road in a residential area. It was a rainy day and it was still dark. A drunk driver hit a minivan and the van flipped several times before landing on its wheels in the center of the road. I took my car and parked it sideways in the road so if another car came along, it would hit my car and not me and the injured people.

The first person I came up to was the driver of the first car. He was dead by the time I got to him. You could smell the alcohol all over him.

Then I walked over to the van and went from person to person and did a normal triage, figuring out which ones I could or couldn't help. The first person I reached was a woman in the driver's seat of the van. I went to her first because she was closest to me. You could tell she was pregnant. She was not breathing and was bleeding, and her face was smothered by the minivan airbag. I did inline stabilization and pulled her body off the airbag. Afterward, she was moving in and out of consciousness, but she was breathing.

When I went to the back seat, I checked out the seven-year-old girl first. She had no breathing and no pulse. But she was trapped in the car, and if I had tried to do CPR, it would not had been effective because of her position. There was just no way I could help her.

I turned my attention to the four-year-old boy in the back seat. He was not breathing, but I was able to get him out of the car. I did rescue breathing for ten minutes and he started to breathe.

I stayed with the family until the EMS arrived. They were there within fifteen minutes, but it seemed like hours. I kept talking to the mother and she would moan and say a couple words. I'd try to tell her to relax, that I'm here, I'll help and the ambulance is on the way.

When I got to work, I came in with blood all over myself and I was wet. I told a co-worker briefly what had happened and that I was going to run to the store to get some clothes. Later that day, I tried to find out what happened to the family, but hospitals are good about not giving out personal information, and the ambulance company couldn't help either. For days I wondered how everything turned out for the family.

A week after the accident, on December 31st, our chapter executive received a letter from the woman. She didn't know my name, but she felt she needed to contact the Red Cross and thank us. I learned that she and her four-year-old son were recovering, and she had delivered a healthy baby girl by Cesarean section the day of the accident. Her seven-year-old daughter had died of her injuries.

Some of the most moving lines in her letter were these: "I don't remember much about the accident but the one memory I do have, as I was waving in and out of awareness, is looking through metal, broken glass, rain and blood to see one individual in a red jacket with a reflective cross and the words American Red Cross on it moving from me then to one of my children and then the another. Though I could not move or talk I remember great pain, but through that I also remember feeling a sense of relief and security that the Red Cross was there."

The letter was the first time anyone had ever tried to find me to thank me. You never hear from most people. You do your thing and the ambulance takes them away.

After twenty-five years of service with the Red Cross, I am often asked why I stay in the same position so long, why I work so many hours under the stress that all of us have. I just tell them stories like that one. Just to have the acknowledgement of what the symbol meant to that woman says it all. You can spend your whole life working and making money, but can you say you make a difference every day? That is why I love being a part of the American Red Cross team.

Kathleen Pearson is responsible for overseeing all lifesaving courses for Middlesex, Mercer and Hunterdon counties in New Jersey, which have a combined population of about 1.3 million residents. At the Central New Jersey chapter, there are more than 1,300 instructors, including "authorized providers" such as Boy and Girl Scout leaders, who were trained by Red Cross instructors, and who teach classes for various local and regional agencies.

Chapter 6

BLOOD BROTHERS

Our ancestors spent considerable blood to ensure that we now have the chance to give a little of it freely as free men and women. We merely urge that you write or telephone your Red Cross chapter and say, "When you want my blood, just let me know." A pint of blood is a small thing to ask. —Edward R. Murrow, in a 1952 documentary called *Biography of A Pint of Blood* on his show, "Hear It Now." On the program, Murrow followed a pint of blood from a donor's arm in the United States to a soldier who underwent surgery at a field hospital in Korea.

In 1940 Dr. Charles Drew, medical director of the first American Red Cross blood bank in the United States, pioneered a method of producing large quantities of dried plasma. His discovery extended the shelf life of blood and made it easier to transport it to troops overseas. Meanwhile, the Red Cross launched a nationwide system of collecting blood that relied on the goodwill of Americans stateside. The organization opened its first blood-donor center in New York City the following February. The next month, mobile units—ten-ton trucks equipped with folding tables, cots and refrigerators—fanned out across communities around the country to collect blood. As the war escalated, volunteer blood donors increasingly rolled up their sleeves. In November

1941 blood collections amounted to about 1,200 pints per week. In December—after the attack on Pearl Harbor—donations jumped to 4,600 pints a week. By the end of April 1942, the weekly donation exceeded 50,000, and by the following September, weekly donations doubled to 100,000, according to the PBS series, *"Red Gold."* By the time World War II ended in 1945, the Red Cross had collected a total of thirteen million pints of blood from more than six million donors. It saved the lives of an unknown number of servicemen.

What began as a vital lifeline for the troops fighting overseas was transformed into a civilian blood program in the post-war era. Blood-mobiles became a fixture in every community and blood drives became widespread. For decades blood collections had been run like a mom and pop store, with friendly Red Cross volunteers who greeted donors and handed out snacks after the donation. The men and women wearing the Red Cross uniform are still there, but just about everything else has changed.

Today, what's called "biomedical services" generate nearly $2 billion in revenues and supplies nearly half of the nation's blood. The blood and blood products are sold to some three thousand hospitals to treat patients, from those undergoing routine surgery to organ and bone-marrow transplant recipients.

COURTESY OF THE AMERICAN RED CROSS

In the past two decades, blood-banking has also been transformed into a tightly regulated industry, largely due to the AIDS epidemic—and it has not been an easy transition. In the 1980s,

more than half of the nation's sixteen thousand hemophiliacs contracted HIV from blood products, according to the CDC, including Ryan
White, the Indiana boy who helped educate Americans about the AIDS
virus. They became infected because both the federal government and
the blood banks—including those operated by the Red Cross—failed
to recognize the magnitude of the AIDS crisis and respond quickly to
protect the blood supply.

In 1991 Senator Elizabeth Dole of North Carolina, then president
of the Red Cross, launched a "transformation" program to improve
the safety of the nation's blood supply. Yet the Red Cross repeatedly
violated blood safety regulations until 1993 when the Food and Drug
Administration (FDA) issued a consent decree ordering the Red Cross
not to collect, process or distribute bad blood.

The late Scott Swisher, M.D., a hematologist whose voluntary Red
Cross service began as a physician on mobile blood collections during
World War II blamed a lot of the initial missteps on poor management.
"Fraud and deliberate deception were not part of the problem," he
said. "Rather, the difficulties were errors of omission, errors of bad
judgment and, in some instances, quite clearly the result of a lack of
sufficient resources and adequate lines of control."

Donna Shalala, as secretary of the department of Health and
Human Services, oversaw the FDA from 1993 to 2001. During that
time, she also served on the Red Cross Board of Governors. She says
that Dole brought tougher management to the Red Cross, which had
been a huge bureaucracy resistant to change. "The improvements were
significant, especially in terms of testing," says Shalala, now president
of the University of Miami. "Cumulatively, the previous presidents of
the Red Cross hadn't dealt with what were fundamental issues—some
related to the quality of the blood supply, and safety concerns."

The number of violations dropped considerably once new testing
systems were put in place, said Dr. Swisher, who was on the Board of
Governors and vice-chairman of the Board's first blood services sub-
committee in the 1980s. "Most of the blood centers—even though they
had lapses—never intentionally allowed the distribution of a unit of
blood that should have been withheld," he said. Instead, most complaints

involved lapses in record-keeping and other procedural errors.

The transformation has been fourteen years in the making, yet the progress has been substantial. More than $300 million was spent to merge the fifty-five local operations across the country into a single national blood system. The organization has also revamped its blood services processing, testing and distribution system, as well as consolidated and upgraded the computer system that maintains the blood-donor database. Eight state-of-the-art national testing labs were opened. To ensure compliance with FDA regulations, a separate department was created to handle quality assurance.

But the long-running battle continues: The FDA again sued the Red Cross in 2002 and another consent decree was signed in the spring of 2003. "We are in what we hope are the final stages of implementing the systems that support that fully integrated national blood system," says former American Red Cross president Marty Evans. She explains that the focus now is making further investments in the IT system and renovating or replacing the thirty-five manufacturing sites with large-volume processing facilities.

As a result of the new directives, donating blood is no longer simply a gift from one person's arm to another. Nowadays, the FDA regulates every step in the blood collection and distribution process. For example, the list of eligibility requirements is extensive—with dozens of possible reasons for exclusion. For example, you can't donate blood if you've had acupuncture or body piercing using an unsterile needle, or take certain medications. "The supply of blood has never been safer," says Evans.

Amidst all the changes, however, one thing remains constant: The Red Cross relies on a faithful cadre of volunteers—four million strong—who show up at regular intervals to donate blood. In fact, only about sixty percent of the nation's population is eligible to donate blood on a given day, and only five percent of those people *ever* give. "We need to figure out how to recruit more donors from across all races and ethnicities, and we need to get them to make a donation more than once a year," says Evans. "Solving that problem is really the holy grail."

Some of the donors, however, have given truly heroic amounts of blood. They often don Red Cross pins that boast how many gallons they have put into the nation's blood bank.

James and Linda Parker of McPherson, Kansas, traveled the United States for a year in 2004 and 2005 donating blood in each of the thirty-six blood service regions, and educating Americans about the need for more blood donors.

For nearly twenty years, Philippe Cournoyer of Worcester, Massachusetts has donated his pheresis—platelets—every two weeks to help cure kids with Leukemia.

Doug Olufsen of Hinesburg, Vermont, has been a blood donor since 1973. For more than fifteen years he has donated pherisis every two to three weeks. "If you're giving whole blood it takes four weeks to regenerate, but because they're only taking platelets my body regenerates them very quickly," explains Olufsen. "I can donate up to twenty-three times a year." All told, he has given seventy-four gallons of blood.

Geoffrey Tatton of Stamford, Connecticut, gives blood every fifty-six days—as often as the law allows. He has been a blood donor for the past three decades. His automobile license plate reads YCSALT—an acronym for the Red Cross motto, "You can save a life, too."

Roy Popkin
Washington, D.C.

It's no coincidence that Roy Popkin chose a career in public relations after attending North Carolina University and New York University. When he was growing up in the Bronx, his father, Louis, was a public relations pioneer in New York, and his mother, Zelda, was an accomplished novelist.

When World War II broke out, twenty-one year old Popkin was working for the British American Ambulance Corps, a war-relief fundraising group in New York. When a medical condition kept him out of the military, he got a job doing public relations for the wartime blood program of the Brooklyn chapter of the American Red Cross.

He stayed with the Red Cross for more than four decades. "All I knew about the Red Cross at that point was that in grade school, you gave a nickel and got a pin with Clara Barton's picture on it," recalls Popkin. "But once I got there, it became my life. Over the years I became so much a part of the organization and it became so much a part of me."

COURTESY OF THE
AMERICAN RED CROSS

Popkin, center, with fellow Red Cross staff members Al Barron and George Petersen standing on the Red Cross ship bound for Cuba in 1963

Back then, the Brooklyn Red Cross was the fourth largest chapter in the country. It was called a "port of embarkation" chapter because we had our volunteers down at the docks seeing the GI's off, giving them comfort kits and welcoming them back when they returned from duty.

Sometimes the Red Cross gave them the first fresh milk they had in years. We had the Navy Yard, the Navy hospital, the Army Terminal and Fort Hamilton, which meant we had all kinds of servicemen going through the place—not only the ones from Brooklyn, but convoys left from the Brooklyn Army Terminal.

Beyond that, the Red Cross was much more proactive as the social services arm of the armed forces. At its peak Brooklyn had 390,000 people in uniform, and that meant all kinds of family problems. We had a staff of about three hundred people running a caseload of about 125,000 a year. A lot of it was emergency furlough stuff, the birth of a child or a death in the family, but we also handled more serious problems.

The head of the program was a marvelous woman named Marion Lounsbury Foster, a well-to-do woman. She didn't need to work, but she was a remarkable social worker. She instilled in the staff the concept that—with this big a caseload—you're going to see the same problem over and over and over again. But even though it's old hat to you, it's not to the families—it's the first time for them. As a result, the Brooklyn chapter gave a very personal service even though at the time, everyone felt overwhelmed.

For example, early in World War II the military did not pay for civilian medical care for family members of the armed forces. We had a woman come in whose husband was a sergeant overseas. She had had seven miscarriages, and she was pregnant again; the doctors told her that if she didn't have this new drug, she would lose the baby, and she would probably never be able to conceive again. She didn't have other children. The drug cost $110 for the whole course of treatment. Today that would be nothing, but that was a lot of money then. She didn't have the cash, and the military wouldn't put it up. So we paid for the medication throughout the whole pregnancy and she had the baby. We got invitations to birthday parties for years.

Blood collections were the biggest challenge. The Red Cross was under contract with the Defense Department. It was called the War Department then. The blood collected was only for the military—we shipped to the laboratories, and the laboratories shipped to the War Department.

Getting new blood donors was difficult. A cadre of blood donors would give blood over and over—we had older people competing for the title of champion blood donor. But we couldn't get the younger people to give blood. They just took the program for granted. It was like social security—somebody had to fight for it once, but now everyone assumes it's there, and that they don't have to do anything about it.

Day after day, we met our quotas through the help of the Brooklyn Dodgers broadcasts. We had a direct line into the press box. When they were broadcasting, we would call periodically during the game and update the announcers, Red Barber and Red Scully, on the schedule and number of donors needed for the next day. They would broadcast it—and they would talk it up. This went on every day there was a game.

You've got to remember what Brooklyn was—it was a community of three million people, and the whole community ethos was wrapped around a ball club—the Brooklyn Dodgers. Most years they were terrible—they were a screwball team—but if the Dodgers won three games in a row, the place was sold out. There was something unique about being a Dodgers fan because we hardly ever won, yet there was a fierce loyalty to the team. Everyone lived and died for the Dodgers. There were guys on the team who lived in Brooklyn, in the neighborhoods, and some of them owned bar and grills. They were part of the community.

I remember the first time the Dodgers as a team came in to give blood, and we gave instructions to the nurses not to take the blood from their throwing arms. Jackie Robinson, Carl Farillo, Pee Wee Reese and Ralph Branca—he was the guy that threw the pitch that lost the playoff game to the Giants in 1951—they all came in right after the season was over or right before it started.

Red Barber would come in and give blood regularly and he would pass out every time. He was a very pale person with red hair and freckles, and you couldn't tell when he would start to faint because he was so fair to begin with. He was a marvelous guy. Ultimately, Red Barber became chairman of the Red Cross fund drive in New York, and he was on the board of the New York chapter.

In 1943, while the war was still on, I was sent to Red Cross national headquarters for a year. At the time, I was also the Washington correspondent for the *Brooklyn Eagle*, the daily newspaper in Brooklyn, once edited by Walt Whitman. We ran the blood program at headquarters with a staff of nine, including secretaries. Now it's a $2 billion-a-year operation. My job was to provide a continuing flow of information to blood centers around the country about the use of plasma. I put out a clipsheet called *Plasma Paragraphs*, which appeared in *Red Cross* magazines. We ran stories of servicemen who were helped by blood transfusions. There were also testimonials from military doctors. I remember one time I had all the medical reports from the invasion of Tarawa, an island in the Pacific, one of the bloodiest invasions of the war—about guys getting transfusions while they were floating in boats in the water.

I stayed in Washington about a year, then came back to Brooklyn. After the war we just kept pounding away at it—finding new ways to recruit blood donors. In 1946, the year after the war ended, I got a call from Jo Ransom, who used to be a columnist for the *Brooklyn Eagle*. Jo read a column on the air on the station that broadcast Dodgers games. He invited all of the radio columnists of the New York papers to the opening day game, and he wanted a gimmick to hand out.

I said that I'd write a first-aid manual for Dodgers fans. It was about two pages long. The theme was "Sit down. Take it easy. Shut up. And to protect yourself and the people around you, take a Red Cross first-aid course."

The idea was that the games could get rowdy. In fact, at one point, just before the war, the Giants were playing the Dodgers up at the Polo Grounds and there was a fight between two players. The Giants were coming into Ebbets Field for three games the following weekend, including a double-header on Saturday, and they expected a riot. The place was loaded with cops, and it was the first time anybody knew of in Major League history that all of the soft drinks were served in paper cups. There wasn't a bottle anyplace except in the press box.

The first-aid manual became a national story. Pauline Frederick, a newscaster on ABC, interviewed me, and several Brooklyn congressmen put the manual into the *Congressional Record*. *Collier's* magazine turned it into an editorial directed at Truman, Stalin and Churchill before the Yalta Conference, and suggested that they follow the advice in our manual.

The next season Ransom wanted another manual, so we did one for lady Dodgers fans. It said, "Wear loose clothing and low heels so as not to get hurt while jumping around." The old *Journal American*, a Hearst afternoon paper, got Carol Channing to come out to Ebbets Field to act it out.

My greatest memory of the Dodgers is in 1951, when the Dodgers got as far as the playoffs with the New York Giants for the National League Championship. Doris Kearns Goodwin wrote a book called *Wait Till Next Year*, and that game is a pivotal part of her book. Anyway, that was the game in which Bobby Thompson of the Giants hit a tenth-inning home run and knocked the Dodgers out of the playoffs. We had the game on television in the blood donor center at the chapter when it happened. And I have this memory that will not go away—of the Red Cross nurses with tears running down their faces as they took needles out of the donors' arms because they were afraid they would go into shock.

In 1957 the Brooklyn Dodgers moved to Los Angeles. In 1960 Roy Popkin again headed to Washington, where he took a job as assistant national director of disaster services at Red Cross national headquarters, and eventually became deputy national director of disaster services.

While in Washington he established the organization's first nationwide disaster public relations system, and he set up a disaster public relations training program. Popkin has been on the scene of scores of disasters from Key West to Alaska. He worked on the Bay of Pigs prisoner exchange and refugee program in 1961 and the Three Mile Island nuclear accident in 1979.

In 1968 Popkin met Mary O'Rourke, public relations director of the Milwaukee chapter of the Red Cross, while he was teaching a Red Cross training course in St. Louis. Two years later, they met again at a conference. They were married in 1971. She moved to Washington and went to work for the Washington, D.C., chapter of the Red Cross before moving over to national headquarters. She retired in 1987.

Popkin retired from the Red Cross in 1984, and works part-time as an editor for the Environmental Protection Agency, where his wife is also employed part-time. He was editor of The Retiree, *a Red Cross newsletter, for nearly a decade and still writes a column for the bi-monthly publication.*

After Hurricane Katrina, Popkin's daughter Gail, a nurse, spent two weeks as a volunteer in Port Sulphur, Louisiana, in Plaquemines Parish. Exactly forty years before, in September 1965, Roy Popkin was stationed in the same parish as a Red Cross disaster relief worker after Hurricane Betsy flooded large parts of New Orleans.

Jean Eshelman
Marietta, Ohio

Jean Eshelman's thirty-one year old son, Russell, died of AIDS in 1992. Russell was born and raised in Marietta, Ohio, a small midwestern town along the Ohio River. At the time he was diagnosed with AIDS he had been living in Fort Lauderdale, Florida, for three years. Russell refused to return to Marietta during his illness because of the stigma attached to the virus in his hometown.

When her son was diagnosed with AIDS in 1990, Eshelman and her husband, Russell's stepfather, were totally uninformed about the virus, and they found few local resources to educate themselves. After Russell's death, Eshelman teamed up with the local Red Cross chapter to help people with AIDS, as well as raise awareness in her community about the virus.

Russell was an intelligent, handsome, beautiful person. He loved his fellow man and enjoyed life to its fullest. He was always smiling and doing for others in every way he could. He was my first-born child, and he was always the big brother to his two younger siblings, a brother and sister. Russell attended Ohio University and had worked in Columbus, Ohio—which is 125 miles from Marietta—for several years prior to moving to Florida.

In 1990, shortly after he moved, he became ill and informed us that

COURTESY OF JEAN ESHELMAN

he was HIV positive—no, it was more than that, he had full blown AIDS. One of the first questions people tended to ask was "How did your son get the virus?" My response was "I don't know, and it is not important—he got it and it took his life." I never asked him myself. It was more important to love him and assure that he got the best care available. A child's sexual orientation or lifestyle is not important when he is critically ill.

We were totally uninformed about the virus. We searched everywhere for information, seeking out anyone who could assist us. We spoke with clergy, human services and a local doctor, and couldn't find anyone who could help us understand the virus. Finally a local priest shared the book *And the Band Played On*. That gave us some insight into what the future would bring.

I spent as much time with Russell as I could during the last twenty months of his life. I traveled frequently to Fort Lauderdale. During the last six months of his life, we moved him into a residential home for persons with AIDS. The home is called Broward House and at the time housed fifty-one other people with AIDS. Most were also terminally ill. There were so many beautiful people there, staff and other residents. The staff was dedicated, kind and loving, with tireless energy and compassion. It was so easy to become close to other residents whose families had disowned them, and wouldn't have anything to do with them because they were infected with the virus. Race, creed and color are not an issue when a mother sees a child in pain. I became very close to three young men in particular, they've all passed now. Seeing parents at Broward House was rare—very few of them were still associated with their children. If a mother spent time there, she became everybody's mother.

Russell passed away on August 12, 1992. He was brought home for the last time to be laid to rest in a country cemetery beside his paternal grandparents. Many of his high school friends came to call, and his brother and brother-in-law gave touching remembrances of the beautiful, loving brother that they had known.

At that time, people with AIDS and their families hid under a rock. There was that much stigma associated with AIDS. That was my first instinct—but I just could not accept Russell's dying in vain. I had heard that there were other people in our small community who had lost their children to the virus and I thought, "Where are they?" I could not find other families, parents or siblings who were willing to share their experiences. But I needed to talk to others who had been there and would understand what I was going through. I refused to accept the "shame" that everyone seemed to harbor. It was unacceptable to me to cast my son and his memory aside because of fear and ignorance.

By late 1993 I couldn't deal with my grief and anger by myself any longer. Late one evening when a friend and I were sitting on the Ohio River levee I said to her, "I am going to do something. I'm not going let this small town make me feel like I've got to hide in shame because my beautiful son contracted a fatal disease."

After numerous phone calls, a health department nurse put me in contact with Jan Packer, executive director of the Washington County Red Cross chapter in Marietta. I met with her and said, "We've got to do something to make this community aware of the effect this disease is having on all of society." She told me that the Red Cross had attempted to put a task force together in prior years but had not been able to get the community's support. But now the time was right, and several of us got together and started an AIDS task force, under the aegis of the Red Cross. We were people with HIV/AIDS, a doctor, a nurse, a nurse practitioner, a teacher, clergy, a journalist and others like myself. The task force was off and running. We held our first World AIDS Day candlelight vigil in 1994. Approximately a hundred and fifty people attended the first one, and vigils were held for five or six years following on World AIDS Day.

We also worked with the Mid-Ohio Valley AIDS task force in Parkersburg, West Virginia. We shared educational trainings and other events, such as planting a tree in memory of all those who have been lost to AIDS, and for those living with it. Local clergy facilitated a weekly support-group meeting for family and friends of persons with HIV/AIDS. We held craft sales to raise funds for HIV/AIDS clients and their immediate families. Most of the individuals with HIV/AIDS in this area have limited economic resources, and so we helped them with housing, clothing and food, as well as funding for medications and transportation to doctors.

Various members of the task force worked with educators, students and parents to provide them with information about the virus. At public forums, the comment you would hear frequently is, "My child is not gay so they do not need to know about HIV/AIDS." Since I was of the same mindset prior to my son's illness, I felt qualified to say, "It's okay for you to feel that way, and I always thought AIDS was going to someone else's house too, but it came to mine. It was devastating—not only did it take my son, it changed the lives of my entire family."

One man I remember especially was the son of someone in my community. He came up to me at one of the candlelight vigils and introduced himself. He said he lived in San Francisco, and he was in town visiting his parents for Christmas. "I'm HIV positive, but I'm not allowed to tell anybody," he said. Then he asked me if I would mind talking to his parents because they were having a difficult time.

I did. The mother was scared to death that her church and the ladies in her circle would find out that her son was gay, and that he had HIV. She thought as long as he stayed in San Francisco nobody would ever know. I kept in touch with him for about three years. He would call every now and then, and he was becoming increasingly sicker. He was so distraught because he wanted to come home, and his mother would have no part of it. When they brought his body back from California, she wouldn't have a service, and she wouldn't let anybody go to the cemetery. My heart has just ached for that lady. It still does because I know how hard it was to accept what had happened. I just don't know how she is ever going to find any peace. And her rejection was so hard on her son.

At that time, I was on a bandwagon. Everywhere I went, I told people, "We've got to learn to accept this virus, and we've got to quit ostracizing families and people with the virus and start looking at it like any other disease." For years, my doctor called me Washington County's AIDS lady. I'm still kind of recognized in some circles as that, and I'm proud of it.

And I'm not the only one anymore. Other mothers and more clergy in the area now are well versed about AIDS. There are more resources. Back when I was searching for somebody to talk to, I didn't know where to go. But that's not true anymore. We even have an infectious-disease doctor in our community now. Ten years ago, that was unheard of. Someone with the virus had to travel to Pittsburgh or Columbus— two- to three-hour drives from here.

We made an impact. I have run into a number of people who have told me if the task force not been around, they never would have come out from under their rock. Parents have become more open to bringing their sick sons and daughters back to the area, and letting them be here for their final days. There is less prejudice than when I lost Russell. We were pretty active for almost six years, but when my husband was diagnosed with cancer in 1999, I quit to care for him. The task force mainly does fundraising now.

I had three children, and I did the PTA bit, my daughter was in a band, my son played football—and I volunteered with the schools and all that. But the work I did at the Red Cross was by far the most rewarding thing I have ever done.

If we weren't associated with the Red Cross—had we gone out on our own and tried to have an AIDS awareness committee or something, it never would have had the impact it did. The town is too small, and the people were just too prejudiced. But being a part of the Red Cross gave us the authority we needed. The Red Cross is still the place that people in Marietta contact if they want information about AIDS.

Jean Eshelman's husband passed away in 2003. The same year, she retired from her accounting job at age sixty-two. In the fall of 2004, Eshelman volunteered with the Red Cross when Marietta experienced the first major flood in forty years. A school in her neighborhood was turned into a makeshift Red Cross shelter. "I have never had any disaster training," she says. "But I just walked across the street and said, 'I'm a Red Cross volunteer—what can I do?'"

Ltc. Jonathon Douglas Bailey, Sr.
Columbus, Ohio

*L*ieutenant Colonel Jonathon Douglas Bailey, Sr., began donating blood in the early 1980s. Needless to say, as an assistant professor of military science at The Ohio State University, and Active Guard and Reservist officer for the Ohio Army National Guard, "Doug" Bailey was also familiar with the services of the American Red Cross. What he didn't realize is that African-American blood donors like himself have been in short supply, which makes it difficult to find blood matches for minority patients.

That changed when Bailey's wife Carla contracted a life-threatening illness that required frequent blood transfusions. Since then, Bailey has become a board member of the Central Ohio Blood Services Region in Columbus, and a member of its diversity task force, one of several Red Cross programs nationwide to educate and recruit minority blood donors. They are in demand because people who require blood transfusions, such as those with blood disorders like sickle-cell disease, fare better if they receive blood donated by a person from the same ethnic or racial background.

While Bailey's wife was still in the hospital, he contacted the Red Cross to see how he could help. "One thing I understand is that life is about service. I feel that God wants us to serve—to love your neighbor as yourself," says Bailey. "The need is out there—and if someone doesn't step up and do something about it, it doesn't get done."

COURTESY OF THE CENTRAL OHIO
BLOOD SERVICES REGION OF
THE AMERICAN RED CROSS

In 2000 my wife Carla contracted a virus called idiopathic thrombocytopenic purpura, or ITP. They don't know how she contracted it. It made her immune system attack its own blood platelets. She required blood because her body was eating it up. It seemed as though every time we turned around, she had to have blood transfusions. She required platelets and occasionally she needed some red blood cells too. Actually, it was infusions, not transfusions. I couldn't even count them because they had to do it so many times.

It got to a point where it was critical—she was on the last thread of life because her body kept rejecting platelets. Finally, her twin sister had plasmaphoresis—that's when they remove the plasma from the blood and sort of scrub the platelets. Her sister's blood is almost identical to hers, so when Carla got her sister's platelets, her body finally accepted them. It slowed down the blood loss and eventually, her health started picking back up.

Carla finally got through the ITP and they were able to stabilize her body from attacking its own platelets. But she started regressing the next year and in 2002 she took a turn for the worse again. She developed congestive heart failure. She was even on a waiting list for a heart transplant. She had just turned forty years old.

That's what got me involved in doing Red Cross blood donations. I started to understand more and more the need for blood—especially the need for ethnic-specific blood. For example, ninety percent of those affected with sickle cell disease are African Americans, and their bodies are more likely to accept blood from other African Americans.

Then I started hearing more statistics about the lack of minority blood donors in general. So I got involved with the diversity task force of the Red Cross. I began looking for opportunities to host or put on blood drives. For example, we put on all-faith, all-denomination, all-city blood drive. The first one was held in 2003 at the Jay Ashburn, Jr., Youth Center in Columbus where I was the executive director at the time. It was a two-day event, Saturday and Sunday. The second year we put it on at the Martin Luther King, Jr., Performing and Cultural Arts Center, another facility in Columbus.

I also became chair of a faith committee that was designed to reach out to the different churches in the community to increase the number of donors from different racial and ethnic backgrounds. We had people from all different parts of the world and all different faiths on the committee—someone from India, someone from Somalia, everything from Christian to Jewish to Muslim. I worked with a Red Cross staff person, Deborah Carvalho, who was really the front person. She and I visited several of the churches and facilities of other faiths to get them involved in blood drives.

By this time I started to tap into other things going on in the African-American community. For example, we—the Red Cross Central Ohio Blood Services Region—have something called the Sickle Cell Donor Program. We try to find donor matches for sickle-cell patients treated at Children's Hospital here in Columbus. When we started, there were only a few, but after we got going, the number of matches increased and that has continued to grow. By 2003 the number of matched donors to sickle cell patients increased from 175 to 450.

My role has been primarily to get more people involved in recruiting minority blood donors—for example, a fraternity, sorority or other groups. I talk to these people and share with them the needs and try to get them committed, and then they recruit among themselves. For example, if you can get someone who's an icon or loved in a church interested, he or she can get others to step up and donate blood.

COURTESY OF THE CENTRAL OHIO BLOOD SERVICES REGION OF THE AMERICAN RED CROSS

Deborah Carvalho, Doug Bailey and Shina Hayden

I never wrote down a campaign plan. Whenever I saw an opportunity to have someone donate blood, I just talked to the person. When I was younger, my grandmother used to say, "People would do better if they knew better." That's my philosophy when I deal with people donating blood—if you personally ask them, most people will donate. Most people do care.

What I did pretty much anybody can do—it's just that someone has to do it. I don't think I did anything hard or anything out of the ordinary. I did it because it's something that needed to be done.

Doug Bailey received the Diversity Ambassador Award at the American Red Cross national convention in 2004. In September 2005, Bailey was called out of retirement and deployed overseas with the military as part of a medical command unit. His wife is fully recovered and volunteers with the American Heart Association.

Karen Mackall
San Diego, California

One week after her seventeenth birthday, Karen Mackall was diagnosed with acute lymphoblastic leukemia (ALL). It is a type of cancer that begins in the bone marrow, and if it's not treated quickly, it can be fatal within months.

Within weeks of the diagnosis, friends, relatives and neighbors rallied round the Mackall family. Karen's mother Ann came up with the idea to do a blood drive—and before long she and Karen teamed up with the Red Cross to hold the first of six blood drives in Karen's name.

During my junior year of high school, I was a swimmer and water polo player. I got hit in water polo in November 2001. You get hit all the time playing water polo, but this time it hurt so much it felt like I couldn't breathe. I couldn't even stay afloat.

A lot of other stuff was going on at the time. For example, I got in a car accident the same month. I was sitting at a red light, and someone hit me from behind going forty-five miles per hour. I got whiplash. Then in January, my grandfather died. I went to the hospital about three times that winter and I'd tell the doctors and nurses about the pain and fatigue I was experiencing, and they'd say, "Oh you're depressed because your grandfather died," or "the pain is from the accident." They did an X-ray and some other tests, but they never took a blood test.

COURTESY OF KAREN MACKALL

On my seventeenth birthday, April 18th, I was on vacation in Hawaii with my family for spring break. I was feeling so lousy, I was screaming in pain. My ribs hurt, and I had really bad chest pains. I felt so bad I didn't even get out of bed. My mom kept saying, "What is the matter with you? Get out of bed—we're in Hawaii."

On the flight back to California, the airline lost our luggage, and we got home really late on a Sunday night. At school the next day, I fainted in my third period class. My parents had gone back to the airport to get our luggage, and the school couldn't reach them. I had a soda in my hand when I fainted, and a girl in my class told our teacher that I had a seizure because I spilled the drink on myself. I said, "No, I think I just fainted."

But since they could not reach my parents, I had to go to the principal's office. The principal asked if I put alcohol in my soda, or if my friend had put it in. I said, "No, her mom is a teacher at the school—we definitely didn't spike our drinks to go to biology class at 10:00 in the morning."

The principal said that because I was seventeen and still a minor and he couldn't contact my parents, he had to have an ambulance take me to the hospital. So I went to the local hospital, San Ramon Regional Hospital. They ran every test possible, *and* they took a blood test.

Finally my mom showed up, about three hours after I got to the hospital. The results came back while we were still there. My blood counts came back really low so they transferred me over to John Muir Medical Center in Walnut Creek that day. The doctor at John Muir said I had aplastic anemia, lupus or leukemia. We had been talking about leukemia during biology class, just before I fainted, so I knew a little about it.

I knew it was leukemia before the doctors told me. They told my parents first and when my parents came into my room, I could tell my dad had been crying. My mom was also crying and she told me that we were going to have a hat party. I remember thinking, *"I don't want a hat party!"*

The doctors said that I probably had had ALL for four months at that point. A day or two later, I went to the University of California at San Francisco Medical Center (UCSF), and started chemotherapy there. They also did several bone marrow biopsies. The beginning was really horrible. I was really, really sick—I don't think I got out of bed for ten days. Plus, a doctor accidentally poked a hole in my lung when he put my catheter in. I was feeling really unlucky by that point. I thought that I was going to die there.

But my treatment went really well. I was what they call an early rapid responder, which means my body responded to the chemo right away, and I went into remission fast. Everything you hear in the beginning, you think it's all going to happen in the next ten days. For example, everyone thought I was going to lose my hair right away. I didn't lose my hair for six months. But when I first got sick, thirteen of my guy friends from high school, my dad and my brother all shaved their heads. They came to see me at UCSF and they were all wearing hats. Then they walked all the way around my bed. And they took off their hats and all of them had shaved heads. My mom just cried.

Within three months of being diagnosed, I participated in my first Red Cross blood drive because there were so many people that wanted to help or donate stuff. People would give my brother and sister rides to school. They brought gifts. They brought meals. We had a room of stuffed animals. I also got a ton of stationery and journals. Finally, I told friends, "Okay, if you guys want to help or do something, you can come and donate blood." This was something that everybody could participate in. You can't have people you know donate blood directly for you, but my goal was just to replace in the blood bank what I used.

The town I grew up in, Danville, is a fairly small town about thirty miles east of San Francisco. At first the Red Cross didn't think many people would turn out. But I had been on the swim team from my neighborhood, Sycamore, starting when I was five until I was eighteen, and I coached it, so we knew many local families. The turnout for the blood drive was tremendous. People stood in long lines and it was very hot that day. A lot of the people who came were scared of needles or worried that it would hurt. I'll never forget this one friend, Erica—she and her mom hate needles. They would wear sunglasses to the blood drives and cry the whole time they gave blood. They still donate blood today. Even my dad would cry when he gave blood. I think donating blood for me affected a lot of people because I was so young—you never think someone that young will get cancer.

So many people came, in fact, that the Red Cross ran out of supplies. They said, "Sorry, we know next time to bring more supplies for *your* blood drive!" Eventually the Red Cross told us our blood drives were so big that they couldn't carry all of the stuff up the stairs at the facility we were using. They needed to find a new place, and we started having the blood drives at a local church, the Community Presbyterian Church. Ultimately we had six blood drives.

The Red Cross made it easy to do them, even the big ones. My mom had a lot to do with it in the beginning. She would take care of most of the big stuff, like getting the costs covered, and securing donations so that the fee for becoming a bone marrow donor, which costs, on average, $70, was waived.

My main job was publicity. My friends and I put up posters everywhere—schools, churches and other places people went around the town. The posters said, "Every one person that donates blood can save three lives." And We would also tell people about the blood drives. Af-

COURTESY OF GENE DAILEY
Karen Mackall, left, at a blood drive in her name

ter the first one, the Red Cross sent out postcards to people who donated at the last drive. While I was at the hospital, I became really close to other families I met there, and a lot of them needed bone marrow. So after the first blood drive, we also did bone marrow registration drives at the same time, even though I never needed bone marrow. All of my friends are in the registry now.

All that's needed for a bone marrow registration is one little vial extra of blood; that gets tested and entered into a registry. There are so many people, like my nurse, who has been in the bone marrow registry for twenty years and has never been called. Very few people ever match with someone who needs a bone marrow transplant. But many people said, "Well, I only want to do it [register as a bone marrow donor] if it goes to Karen." What a stupid thing to say! I would say, the relationship I have with you, someone else has that with someone else—someone else who is a donor." If everybody could think of it that way, there would be a lot more blood and bone marrow donors out there.

I wish that I could donate blood but I don't think I ever can because I had chemotherapy, but I feel like I made a contribution. People tell me all the time, "I still donate blood every eight weeks ever since your blood drive." Or they say, "I went and donated blood and I thought of you."

Although Karen Mackall was absent several weeks of school during her senior year, she graduated from Monte Vista High School with her class in 2002. Mackall attended Diablo Valley Junior College and lived at home while she was still undergoing treatment. She and her mother organized a highly successful blood and bone marrow drive at the junior college.

During "maintenance"—the final stage of chemotherapy—Mackall swam on the swim team and played water polo. She participated in the first of two triathlons called The Treasure Island Triathlons in San Francisco and the Wildflower Triathlon in San Luis Obispo. She also trained with Team-In-Training to raise money for the Leukemia & Lymphoma Society.

Karen Mackall finished treatment for ALL in 2003, and transferred to San Diego State University, where she is studying to become a nurse.

My Red Cross Story

Acknowledgements

I am most grateful to the twenty-nine Red Cross staff and volunteers who gave freely of their time and shared their stories and memories with me. Special thanks to Roy Popkin, Ross Ogden, Warren Zorek and Pete Ashen for their advice and assistance. I am also indebted to the dozens of other staff and volunteers who gave generously of their time and knowledge over the past two years.

The book never would have been written without the support of the "believers" who encouraged me early on to write, Ken Curtin and the late Scott Swisher. And it wouldn't look nearly as good if Gene Dailey, photographer and volunteer extraordinaire, hadn't allowed me to use his wonderful images.

Of course, the support of Red Cross national headquarters has been invaluable in ensuring that I captured what the Red Cross means to its staff and volunteers, and to all Americans. Except where otherwise noted in the text, I owe the statistics and facts relating to Red Cross activities to the American Red Cross and the International Red Cross and Red Crescent Societies.

Special thanks to Darren Irby, Chuck Conner and Marisa Frank. Several other staff members lent their expertise and assistance: Tara Lynch, Jeffrey Hon, Carol Miller, Ashley Young, Brook Urban, Anita Foster, Erika Mayor, Catherine West, Greg Smith, Peter Teahen, Debby Hampton and Nancy Retherford. I am particularly indebted to Susan Watson and Tom Goehner in the Historical Resources Department, as well as Betty Wagner in the Retirees' office and Anita Wright of ARCOA.

To friends and family members who lent a hand or an ear: Amey Stone, Mike Brewster, Dawn Margolis, Deb Forhan, Mary Beth

Donahue, Emi Macuaga and Tom Gallagher. Thanks also to colleagues in the publishing industry who advised me: Paul Bresnick, Kerri Smith, Winifred Conkling and Phil Whitmarsh.

I am indebted to the team who worked on the book: technical advisor Mindy McKeown, copy editor Sarah Burns, and attorney Nina Graybill. I am so fortunate to have met Lauren Clayton, who worked magic with the images; Liz Tufte, who worked tirelessly through the holidays to design the interior; and Bob Aulicino for a striking cover design. Also thanks to helpers Nora Hammerman, Sarah Carter and Nicole Weisenburger.

Above all, my deepest thanks to Lorraine Dusky, who grasped the promise of this project and helped turn my idea into a book. Her advice and commitment to the book have been invaluable. Of course, to my husband Russ, who has been supportive and understanding— not realizing how long the gestation would be. Finally, to my parents, who never stop telling me how important it is to give, and my children, who picked up on that lesson too.